· Executive Severance ·

Jane Kissack
Solicitor, Eversheds

Stephen Hart
Solicitor, Simmons & Simmons

Christopher Walter
Associate, Baker & McKenzie

Palladian Law Publishing Ltd

© Jane Kissack
Stephen Hart
Christopher Walter
1999

Published by
Palladian Law Publishing Ltd
Beach Road
Bembridge
Isle of Wight PO35 5NQ

www.palladianlaw.com

ISBN 1 902558 08 1

Neither Jane Kissack, Stephen Hart, Christopher Walter nor Palladian Law Publishing Ltd shall be liable for any loss, damages, claims, demands, expenses or other liability, whether direct or indirect, incurred by any person in connection with this work howsoever arising.

The right of Jane Kissack, Stephen Hart and Christopher Walter to be identified as the authors of this work has been asserted in accordance with the Copyright, Designs and Patents Act 1988

Typeset by Heath Lodge Publishing Services
Printed in Great Britain by The Book Company Limited

· Contents ·

Preface   vii
About the Authors   viii
Table of Cases   ix
Table of Statutes   xi

1   **Introduction**
What's on the horizon   1
Fairness at work   1
Woolf reforms   2
How it went wrong   3

2   **Dismissal: a thorough grounding**
What is a dismissal?   5
Potential grounds for dismissal   6
Constructive dismissal   17
Reasonableness   23
Key points   29

3   **Preparations for dismissal**
What do you want?   31
Is the executive a director?   31
Is the executive a shareholder?   34
Impact of contract on termination as an employee   35
Sample clauses   36

4   **How are we getting there?**
Introduction   39
Strategy   39
Negotiations and other issues   40
Key points   46

5   Documenting the deal: the severance agreement
    Introduction   48
    Types of severance agreement   48
    What is a compromise agreement?   49
    Role of ACAS and arbitration   59
    Key points   60

6   Costing the deal
    Introduction   62
    What are the legal claims?   62
    Assessing the value of severance package   72
    General principles   73
    Assessing lost remuneration   77
    Other claims/heads of loss   85
    Further increasing value of severance package   87
    Taxation of severance payment   90
    Mitigation/accelerated receipt   96
    Key points   98

7   Protection of business interests
    Introduction   99
    Activities while employed   100
    Activities after employment   110
    Key points   117

    Appendix A: Letter confirming dismissal   121
    Appendix B: Garden leave clause   122
    Appendix C: Compromise agreement   123
    Appendix D: Calculation of wrongful dismissal damages 129
    Appendix E: Letter of resignation of directorship(s)   131

    Index   133

· Preface ·

When considering the termination of employment of a senior employee, the decision itself is often divorced from the process. In other words, employers may have a very clear idea what it is they want to achieve, but are unclear how to get there.

Where the process is mishandled the consequences for both employer and employee can be disastrous. The senior employee (or "executive" as they are generally referred to in this book) may be forced to litigate with his ex-employer to whom many years' long service may have been devoted. Relations with former colleagues are soured and time and money are needlessly expended by both parties. The employer, on the other hand, discovers that the cost of misreading contractual provisions, or overlooking procedural safeguards can be prohibitive. Morale among the workforce generally may suffer. Ex-employees are also often in a position to damage external business interests where they feel aggrieved at the manner in which their employment was terminated.

The purpose of this book is therefore to provide employers with an overview of the issues and material to be reviewed before effecting the termination of an executive's employment. Practical guidance is also given in relation to procedural safeguards, calculations of severance payments, preparation of compromise agreements, protection of business interests and so on.

Preparation is crucial, but employers also need to be flexible. For the executive, a dismissal can be an extremely traumatic event. The process will be so much less painful for him when it is handled efficiently and when arrangements proposed (including financial offers, internal and external statements, on-going benefits etc) reflect the rights and wrongs of each situation.

We would particularly like to thank Dan Perrett of Eversheds for his input into the book.

Jane Kissack
Stephen Hart
Christopher Walter
London, July 1999

· About the Authors ·

Jane Kissack

Jane Kissack joined Eversheds in 1994, after reading Modern History at Oxford and gaining a distinction in the Legal Practice Course. She is a member of Eversheds' employment and pensions group and regularly advises on high profile mergers and reorganisations, as well as her own specialist field of employment contracts, service and consultancy agreements and executive severance matters.

Stephen Hart

Stephen Hart qualified as a solicitor in 1995 and joined the London office of Eversheds, specialising in employment law. He has acted for a wide range of corporate, individual and public sector clients, dealing with severance, unfair dismissal, redundancies, contractual issues and discrimination. In 1999, he moved to the City practice of Simmons & Simmons to join their employment team.

Christopher Walter

Christopher Walter was called to the Bar at Lincoln's Inn in 1991, after studying at City University. He re-qualified as a solicitor in 1994 and has since specialised in the field of employment law, with particular emphasis on business reorganisations and acquisitions, transfer issues and redundancy. In 1999, he joined the employment department of Baker & McKenzie having spent almost three years in the London office of Eversheds.

· Table of Cases ·

Addis v Gramophone Company [1909] AC 488, HL   86
Armitage, Marsden & HM Prison Service v Johnson [1997] IRLR
     162, EAT   71

BBC v Beckett [1983] IRLR 43, EAT   20
BET v Clark [1997] IRLR 348   64, 75, 77, 78, 79, 84
Balston Ltd v Headline Fitters Ltd [1990] FSR 385   103
Bevan Harris Ltd v Gair [1981] IRLR 520, EAT   24

Chapman v Aberdeen Construction Group plc [1991] IRLR 505   84

D v M [1996] IRLR 192   94
Digital Equipment Co Ltd v Clements (No 2) [1998] IRLR 425   68

Faccenda Chicken Ltd v Fowler [1987] Ch 117; [1986]
     ICR 297 [1986] IRLR 69, CA   100

Grootcon (UK) Ltd v Keld [1984] IRLR 302, EAT   16

Heggie v Uniroyal Englebert Tyres Ltd [1998] IRLR 425   68
Henderson v Granville Tours Ltd [1982] IRLR 494, EAT   24
Hillman v London General Transport Services Ltd, EAT, April 1999   14

James v Waltham Holy Cross UDC [1973] IRLR 202   10
Janciuk v Winerite Ltd [1998] IRLR 63, EAT   87

King v The Great Britain – China Centre [1991] IRLR 513; [1992]
     ICR 516, CA   28

Lavarack v Woods of Colchester [1967] QB 278, CA   75
Levett v Biotrace International plc, *The Times*, May 1999, CA   85

Mahmud v Bank of Credit and Commerce International SA [1997]
     ICR 606, HL   19
Mairs v Haughey [1993] IRLR 551, HL   92

Malik v Bank of Credit and Commerce International [1997]
    IRLR 462   21, 64, 85
Micklefield v SAC Technology Ltd [1990] 1 All ER 275   84
Midland Bank plc v McCann, 23 July 1998, EAT   79
Morris Angel & Son Ltd v Hollande [1993] ICR 71; [1993]
    IRLR 169, CA   114

Nicholson v Budget Insurance Ltd, 8 June 1998, EAT   87
Noble Enterprises Ltd v Lieberum, June 1998, EAT   79

O'Laoire v Jackel International Ltd [1990] IRLR 70   70

Polkey v A E Dayton Services Ltd [1988] AC 344; [1987]
    3 WLR 1153; [1988] ICR 142; [1987] 3 All ER 974; [1987]
    IRLR 503, HL   25, 26
Provident Financial Group v Hayward [1989] ICR 160, CA   106

Roberts v Elwell Engineers Ltd [1972] 2 QB 586   78

Safeway Stores plc v Burrell [1997] ICR 523, EAT   12
Sawicki v Computacenter Ltd (1998), EAT   51
Seymour Smith, HL (awaiting judgment)   2
Shove v Downs Surgical plc [1984] ICR 532   63, 76, 80, 93
Skyrail Oceanic Ltd t/a Goodmos Tours v Coleman [1980]
    IRLR 226, EAT   15

Taupo Totoro Timber Co Ltd v Rowe [1978] AC 537   73
Treganowen v Robert Knee & Co Ltd [1975] ICR 405; [1975]
    IRLR 247   16

Wallace Bogan v Cove [1997] IRLR 453   101
Western Excavating (EEC) Ltd v Sharp [1978] QB 761; [1978]
    IRLR 27, CA   18, 22
Whittle Contractors Ltd v Smith EAT 842/94   81, 109
William Hill Organisation Ltd v Tucker [1998] IRLR 313, CA   108
Winterhalter Gastronom Ltd v Webb [1973] IRLR 120   10

· Table of Statutes ·

Companies Act 1985
    s 303 — 33
    s 317 — 14
    s 459 — 35
Employment Rights Act 1996
    8, 93
    s 98(4) — 23
    s 139 — 11
    s 203 — 49, 65

Employment Rights (Dispute
Resolution) Act 1998 — 49, 89
    s 13 — 67

Income and Corporation Taxes Act
1988
    s 19 — 90, 91, 92
    s 148 — 91, 92, 93
    s 313 — 93
    s 579 — 92
    Sched 11 — 91, 92

Restrictive Trade Practices Act
1976 — 114

Trade Union & Labour Relations
(Consolidation) Act 1992 — 13

Chapter 1

· **Introduction** ·

What's on the horizon?

In this book the term "executive" has been used to described individuals engaged both as directors and employees of their employer (which it has generally been assumed would be a company). They may also be shareholders and, before effecting a dismissal, each of these roles should be considered separately. In terms of the employment relationship there are four questions to be asked at the outset:

(1) Why is the company deciding to dismiss this executive?
(2) What are the contractual implications of the decision under the agreements governing the company's relationship with the executive?
(3) What are the statutory implications?
(4) Who will effect the dismissal, and does that person have authority to do so?

It may seem obvious, but it is often forgotten that, even where there are clear grounds for dismissing an executive (where, for example, there has been an obvious attempt to undermine the company's interests, in breach of the employment contract) a dismissal is likely to become protracted and costly if reasonable procedures are not followed. Alternatively, where the company really does not have evidence to support an argument that the executive has breached fundamentally his employment contract, that fact should be recognised and the approach to dismissal planned accordingly. Recent developments in the law underline the importance of preparation, since serious consequences could result from the mishandling of executive terminations in the future.

"Fairness at Work"

Following its Fairness at Work White Paper in its subsequent Employment Relations Bill, the Government has proposed that the ceiling on the compensatory award in the employment tribunal be raised to £50,000. In addition, the Government has with effect from 1 June 1999 reduced the period of qualifying service for unfair dismissal from two years to one.

Even prior to this, dismissed executives with continuous employment of more than one year were entitled to a stay of employment tribunal proceedings until the House of Lords rules in the case of *Seymour Smith* on whether the two–year qualifying period was discriminatory and contravened European law.

Given these extensions of employment rights, the executive will be able to seek a low cost and quick remedy for unfair dismissal, with compensation more realistically reflecting his loss than was previously the case. The executive also has the advantage that, in the employment tribunal, each side bears its own costs regardless of the outcome of the case (unless one or other side has been unreasonable in the conduct of the case or where the claim is frivolous or vexatious). The executive may have nothing to lose, therefore, in issuing unfair dismissal proceedings where a termination has been handled badly.

The Woolf reforms

In April 1999, following the proposals of Lord Woolf, the civil justice system and court rules were subject to a series of sweeping changes designed to make litigation less complicated and to encourage settlement.

In the context of termination of an executive's employment, these reforms relate to the executive's contractual claims. Statutory claims will continue to be subject to the employment tribunal's jurisdiction.

In practice, the reforms will require both parties to be more open with each other even before proceedings are issued, to disclose relevant documents voluntarily and actively to pursue settlement. For employers and their advisers this will mean changes to the way in which cases are run, negotiations conducted and dismissals are effected.

The reforms will impact significantly on settlement negotiations. If the aim is to demonstrate that efforts have been made to settle claims, to lessen the risk to the company of cost awards against it, it will be advisable for the company to make a sensible settlement offer. The key to successful negotiations therefore is an early assessment of the company's liabilities, its chances of successfully defending any claim and any possible counterclaims against the executive.

The Woolf reforms will also mean that the court will be able to decide on issues relevant to the case and to call upon parties to discard irrelevant points or those which have little chance of success. The cynical company will be less able to "throw mud" at an executive, secure in the knowledge that it has deeper pockets for a protracted legal battle. Equally, it will be far more risky simply to dismiss an executive and challenge him to issue proceedings since the company may be called upon by the court to justify its decision far earlier than at trial and may find its defence and counterclaim struck out where its legal position is unsustainable.

It is increasingly important for companies to get their procedures correct and, when faced with dismissing an executive, to work out in advance the potential costs of the severance, the likelihood of litigation and the appropriate approach to take in the light of those considerations. As the threat of litigation becomes more serious, the "best practice" dismissal may be the best means of saving the company time and costs.

How it went wrong

The sort of mistakes which can easily arise when effecting a termination are illustrated by the following example.

The company in this case employed B as its marketing director. Under B's contract he was entitled to 12 months' notice of the termination of his employment, when he would be obliged to resign his directorship and return all company property, including his company car. B was also a shareholder in the company.

The board had lost confidence in B, who had under-performed (although not significantly), and was not motivating the sales team. However, these concerns had never been raised with him, and the evidence was more anecdotal than factual. As a result, the board decided to dismiss B and wrote him a letter simply informing him that his employment would terminate with immediate effect. No mention was made of B's directorship, and the company was clearly acting in breach of the contractual obligation to provide notice. At the same time, B was given an indication that he should approach a lawyer so that negotiations could commence. This comment was not made "without prejudice" and so could be used against the company at court as evidence that the company knew it was doing wrong. It was also, of course, inviting a fight.

B refused to leave. His solicitor faxed the company pointing out that they were purporting to terminate B's contract in breach (which, if it were accepted, would also be unfair) but that B would not accept such a breach and expected the company to continue to honour its contractual obligations to B. B continued to turn up at the office, to contact customers of the company and arrange team meetings, which was exceedingly embarrassing for all concerned and damaging to company interests. Unfortunately, the company did not have security staff to prevent B turning up at the office, nor could they simply cancel a security pass.

As a matter of law B could not enforce the employment relationship, but the company was faced with a difficult practical problem, which may have been avoided with planning. Following negotiations between lawyers for B and the company, B agreed to go on garden leave and the company withdrew its purported letter of termination, while negotiations commenced over a severance package. B refused to resign his directorship, because he was not contractually obliged to do so until the end of his employment, and claimed that he was being prejudiced as a minority shareholder, contrary to section 459 of the Companies Act 1985. The cost, in terms of both legal fees and management time, was very substantial and staff morale was lowered considerably by the unfortunate events.

Had an appropriate offer been made to B in the first place, recognising his rights as an employee and shareholder, and the absence of adequate grounds for dismissal, it is likely that he would have agreed to a short period of absence from the office while negotiations were conducted. It may have been possible to reach agreement quickly, with B agreeing to waive his claims against the company, agreeing announcements, return of company property, appropriate payments and so on.

Chapter 2

Dismissal: A Thorough Grounding

Where there are no grounds for instant dismissal the company's principal aim will usually be to agree terms governing the termination, so that it is effectively a mutually agreed departure rather than a dismissal. However, that is not always achievable and the company may be faced with the prospect of dismissing the executive and then fighting claims. To enhance the company's negotiating position and give it the best chance of defending potential claims it is important to understand what amounts to a dismissal at law, and the grounds available to the company for effecting a fair and reasonable dismissal.

2.1 What is a dismissal?

Dismissal occurs in the following circumstances:

- the executive's contract of employment is terminated by the company, with or without notice. In order for the termination to be effective, there must be a clear and unambiguous statement to that effect;
- where the executive is employed under a fixed term contract, he is dismissed when the term of the contract expires and it is not renewed;
- where the executive resigns his employment with or without notice in response to the company's conduct. Where, for example, the executive has been forced to resign because the alternative would be dismissal, the law treats this as a dismissal. Similarly, where the company has breached fundamentally any term of the executive's employment contract, he would be entitled to resign without notice and claim constructive dismissal. These issues are addressed in greater detail below.

2.2 **Potential grounds for dismissal**

When effecting a dismissal, the company should consider the executive's contractual and statutory rights. These issues interrelate to a great extent, and the various fair grounds for dismissal, under the Employment Rights Act 1996, are therefore considered below, with consideration given to contractual implications in each case. While until recently executives with less than two years' service were not entitled to claim unfair dismissal, it has been assumed in this chapter that statutory as well as contractual rights will be a concern to the company, for the reasons outlined in the introduction.

The five potentially fair reasons for a dismissal are:

(1) Conduct
(2) Capability
(3) Redundancy
(4) Illegality
(5) "Some other substantial reason."

Conduct

There are a number of possible ways in which conduct could lead to dismissal.

Employment contract

The issue of conduct may arise under the executive's contract of employment which will commonly contain the following express obligations:

- to provide services exclusively to the employing company;
- to promote the company's interests to the best of his ability;
- to respect the confidentiality of information received by him during his employment;
- to perform his duties with appropriate care and skill;
- to comply with the company's reasonable and lawful requests;
- to perform services for group companies, where reasonably requested to do so;
- to comply with expenses procedures.

Breach of such contractual obligations may provide grounds for termination.

Contracts will also usually contain a non-exhaustive list of grounds for instant dismissal (including gross misconduct, such as drunkenness, violence, or harassment, serious breach of duty, bankruptcy, disqualification from directorship etc).

Conduct falling below the standard of that to be expected of an executive may justify the company in taking disciplinary action against him leading, ultimately, to dismissal. The company's principal obligation in such circumstances is to comply with the statutory obligation to act reasonably in accordance with any procedures operated by the company (see 2.4, below).

Gross misconduct

Gross misconduct is conduct which is so serious that it amounts to a fundamental breach of the executive's contractual obligations to the company. The breach goes to the heart of the contractual relationship between the executive and the company, justifying instant dismissal. As indicated above, executive employment contracts commonly provide for summary termination where the executive has committed an act of gross misconduct.

A serious breach of an implied duty, such as the fiduciary duty owed by directors referred to below, or the general obligation imposed on both the company and executive not to act in a way which undermines trust and confidence between them, may be a reason justifying summary dismissal.

Where the executive is guilty of gross misconduct, his employment contract may be terminated without notice or a payment in lieu of notice. There are, however, two important qualifications to this:

(1) The company should check the executive's employment contract to see whether there are references to a disciplinary procedure. Where a disciplinary procedure is incorporated into the executive's employment contract, a failure to follow the procedure will be a breach of contract, and the executive may claim damages for the period during which his employment would have subsisted while the procedure was followed. It is also theoretically possible that the executive may claim far greater damages where he could establish that, had the contractual procedure been followed, he would have remained employed by the company. So far the courts have not been prepared to award damages on this basis (see Chap 6). On rare occasions, employees have also successfully injuncted their employer to ensure that they follow contractual procedures relating

to dismissal. For the above reasons, therefore, the company should either comply with contractual procedures, or amend contracts to remove them;

(2) The company is under an obligation under the Employment Rights Act 1996 to act reasonably. As a minimum this means that there should be a proper investigation, that the executive should be given a fair opportunity to answer the allegations against him, and that proper consideration should be given to the evidence against the executive and his explanation before a decision is made. Under the Employment Relations Bill it is proposed that executives should be entitled to be accompanied at disciplinary hearings, either by a work colleague, or a union representative. This requirement will apply to every level of employee. These issues are explored in greater detail below.

Directors' duties – common law/contractual

If the executive is a director of the company, the executive owes fiduciary duties to the company. Two aspects of this fiduciary duty are particularly relevant:

(1) **Duty to act in good faith.** A director has a duty to act in what he considers to be the best interests of the company and not for any other purpose. Providing that he maintains this standard and can show he has acted in the company's best interests, he discharges his duty. The courts will allow the director absolute discretion, interfering only if it believes that the director's actions were such that no reasonable director could have believed that the course of action was in the best interests of the company. The courts do not expect the executive always to be right and recognise that senior management occasionally has to take risks. However, where the director acts honestly but not in the best interest of the company, he will nevertheless be in breach of this duty.

It should also be noted that the executive may be at risk of breaching this duty if he is asked to and approves a particularly generous or complex severance package, or agrees to the dismissal of a fellow director whose role was critical to the company's success.

(2) **Conflicts of interest.** A director must not put himself in a position where there is an actual or potential conflict between his personal interest and his duties to the company.

Directors have both a fiduciary duty and a statutory duty under section 317 of the Companies Act 1985 to make a full disclosure to the board of any potential or actual conflicts between their personal interests and their duties as directors. This duty extends to any employment contract or consultancy agreement between the company and a director.

Capability

While it will be an obligation of the executive to perform his duties with appropriate care and skill, it is not common for a company to be able to dismiss an executive summarily for poor performance. In such cases the company would have to show gross negligence.

Capability issues may either arise where the executive simply cannot perform to the required standard (despite his best efforts) or where the executive is unwilling to perform to the required standard. The company will be justified in dismissing the executive on either grounds (provided it is acting reasonably in doing so) but the approach adopted may be quite different. For example, it is increasingly common for disciplinary procedures to be employed for under-performance as well as misconduct.

General principles – tried but can't

- Has the executive's performance been measured objectively?
- Have any possible reasons for departure from a normally satisfactory standard been taken into account?
- Has the executive been made aware of the shortcomings in his performance? Are targets set realistic and achievable?
- Has consideration been given to additional training?
- Was the executive warned of the consequences of a continued failure to perform adequately?

General principles – can but won't

- Has the executive been given clear guidance as to the standard expected? Were those targets realistic and achievable?
- Has the position been properly monitored and are the results reliable?
- Has the executive been given an opportunity to explain the under-performance?

- Was the executive warned of the consequences of a continued failure to perform?
- Has the company complied with any disciplinary procedures?

Executives and formal warnings

For senior employees in particular there has been a tendency for the tribunal to say that there will frequently be no need to give them a specific warning that their jobs are in jeopardy. This will often be clear from the circumstances. In *James* v *Waltham Holy Cross UDC* [1973] IRLR 202 Sir John Donaldson commented:

> " ... Those employed in senior management may by the nature of their jobs be fully aware of what is required of them and fully capable of judging for themselves whether they are achieving that requirement. In such circumstances the need for warning and an opportunity for improvement are much less apparent."

The cases suggest that the executive should normally, by virtue of his position, be aware that his job is in peril. However, in some circumstances this may not be clear. In the case of *Winterhalter Gastronom Ltd* v *Webb* [1973] IRLR 120 a sales director was dismissed because of poor sales results, though at no time had he been given any warning. The employment tribunal found the dismissal to be unfair. In rejecting an argument that a warning can never be appropriate in a capability case, Sir Hugh Griffiths said:

> "We do not agree. There are many situations in which a man's apparent capabilities may be stretched when he knows what is being demanded of him; many do not know that they are capable of jumping the five-barred gate until the bull is close behind them. No doubt there may be cases in which giving a warning to a director would be neither necessary nor achieve any useful purpose. But each case must depend upon its own particular facts and it is, in the view of this court, quite impossible to say as a matter of law that there can never be circumstances in which it is necessary to give a warning to a director before dismissing him."

Given this and in the light of the raised cap for unfair dismissal compensation, employers should put in place procedures to deal with the under-performance of executives. However, this could be an abbreviated version of the procedures applied to junior staff.

Redundancy

The definition of redundancy set out in section 139 of the Employment Rights Act 1996 provides that an executive is taken to be dismissed by reason of redundancy if the dismissal is wholly or mainly attributable to:

- the fact that the company has ceased or intends to cease to carry on the business for the purposes of which the executive was employed by it, or to carry on that business in the place where the executive was so employed;
- the fact that the requirements of that business for executives to carry out work of a particular kind, or for executives to carry out work of a particular kind in the place where the executive was employed by the company, have ceased or diminished or are expected to cease or diminish.

Redundancy is a fair ground for dismissal, subject, again, to the company's obligation to act reasonably. A detailed outline of the law relating to redundancy is beyond the scope of this book, but it is useful to consider briefly the three principal types of redundancy.

Closure of business

Complete closure of the business is the most obvious redundancy situation. A change of the type of business conducted by the company may also be regarded as a closure of the old business where the new business is sufficiently different.

Closure of workplace

The relevant part of the section requires that the company must cease or intend to cease to carry on the business in the "place where the executive was ... employed". The tribunal will consider all the relevant facts of the case in determining the place of employment, not just the contract of employment. If the executive has, in fact, worked at a number of different locations, however, the terms of the contract (including any mobility clause) will be relevant in determining the place of employment and, hence, the existence or otherwise of a redundancy situation.

Diminishing need for executives

This covers the situation where work of a particular kind has diminished, so that the executive has become surplus to requirements. It also applies where work has not diminished but fewer executives are needed to do the work, either because the executives have been replaced by, say, independent contractors or advances in technology. In the case of *Safeway Stores plc v Burrell* [1997] ICR 523, EAT the Employment Appeals Tribunal (EAT) set out a three–stage test:

- was the executive dismissed?
- had the requirements of the company's business for executives to carry out work of a particular kind ceased or diminished, or were they expected to do so?
- if so, was the dismissal caused wholly or mainly by the cessation or diminution?

This decision shifted the focus from the position of the particular executive to the company's needs in a general sense and the operative cause of the dismissal.

In the event of a redundancy, the company will need to give consideration to the following issues:

The right to a statutory redundancy payment

Statutory redundancy payments are calculated by multiplying the number of full years worked by weekly wage (currently up to a maximum of £220), by a factor allowing for age (0.5 for years worked between the ages of 18 and 21, one for years worked between the ages of 21 and 41 and 1.5 for subsequent years worked to the age of 60) (see also Chap 6). It is common for larger companies to make enhanced redundancy payments, which include statutory payments due to executives. Such payments may amount to an express contractual entitlement. Alternatively, where companies have been through a number of redundancy exercises and consistently operated an unwritten policy, it is also possible that executives may argue that they have an implied contractual right to enhanced payments or to a given procedure (on the basis of custom and practice). Companies should therefore check redundancy policies/procedures, and the practice adopted in previous redundancy exercises, in order to ensure that a failure to provide enhanced payments or to follow a given procedure would not give rise to claims for breach of contract.

Consultation

In a redundancy case, the company is (with extremely limited exceptions) under an obligation to consult with individuals in relation to the following issues:

- reason for the redundancy;
- explanation of the pool for selection;
- the selection criteria;
- reason for selection for redundancy;
- availability of alternative employment.

How far does this individual consultation need to go in the case of executives? An executive may often be better placed to appreciate the reasons for redundancies. In the case of redundancies resulting from a merger, for example, which affect the executive, he may already be aware of the need for and the economic rationale behind the redundancies. Therefore, many of the above points will already be obvious to the executive. In addition, where the executive is one of 20 or more employees at one establishment that the company proposes to dismiss as redundant within a period of 90 days or less, the company is under a statutory obligation to consult on a collective basis with either recognised trade unions or elected employee representatives (Trade Union and Labour Relations (Consolidation) Act 1992). Consultation must be undertaken with a view to reaching agreement on ways of avoiding the dismissals, or reducing the numbers affected and mitigating the consequences of the dismissals.

Illegality

The company can in principle fairly dismiss an executive where it can show "that the employee could not continue to work in the position which he held without contravention (either on his part or that of his employer) of a duty or restriction imposed by or under any enactment." The continued employment must in fact contravene a statutory enactment; it is not enough that the company genuinely believes this to be the case.

The company must still act reasonably and it is unlikely to meet that requirement if it refuses to make modifications to the executive's job that would accommodate the prohibition.

In order to satisfy the reasonableness test (see 2.4, below), the company may have to consider offering the executive any alternative employment that is available, particularly if he is long-serving.

Furthermore, it should consider alternative methods of doing the work which would not be unlawful.

In the context of senior employment, examples of relevant prohibitions include:

- where the executive fails to disclose any direct or indirect interest that he has in any contract or proposed contract with the company, in contravention of section 317 of the Companies Act; and
- where a work permit or other immigration clearance (required under the Asylum and Immigration Act 1996) for the executive to work in the United Kingdom, is refused, lapses or is withdrawn.

Some other substantial reason

A dismissal may also be fair if the company can show that it is "for some other substantial reason of a kind such as to justify the dismissal of an employee holding the position which the employee held." Provided the reason is substantial and not whimsical, it is capable of falling under this heading. Again, the company must act reasonably in treating the reason as sufficient to justify dismissal (see 2.4, below).

Although the category is potentially open-ended, most of the fair dismissals under this heading arise because the company is taking action to protect business interests. It may be that it wishes to reorganise, or prevent the publication of confidential information to a competitor, or restrict the opportunity for executives to resign and set up in competition. These changes generally necessitate the executive accepting a change in the terms and conditions of his employment, and it is his refusal to accept this change which may bring about his dismissal (either actual or constructive).

Changes to terms and conditions

In the case of *Hillman* v *London General Transport Services Ltd*, EAT, April 1999, the applicant was employed by the company and was one of two staff who refused to accept new and less favourable terms of employment which had been negotiated between the company and the MYX. The changes resulted from the withdrawal of block funding and the company's desire to have some chance in the process of competitive tendering for routes operated by London Transport. The applicant had been warned that if he did not agree, his employment would be terminated on 12 weeks' notice. He complained of unfair dismissal but the tribunal was satisfied that the company had some other substantial reason justifying the dismissal and that the company had acted reasonably in all respects.

Recent decisions therefore lean heavily in favour of upholding management's right to reorganise the business in a manner which it considers advantageous. However, it is subject to two important limitations which impose some restrictions on that prerogative.

(1) The company must demonstrate that the reorganisation/changes have discernible advantages.
(2) The interests of executives cannot be ignored when a tribunal is determining whether the company has a sound, business reason for the dismissal. Whether the company has acted properly in all the circumstances in seeking to impose the change will depend, at least in part, on whether the executive acted reasonably in refusing the change.

An important factor which in practice affects the tribunal's assessment of whether a dismissal is fair is the extent to which the proposed reorganisation is agreed following negotiations with any recognised trade union or employee representatives. This will in practice be powerful evidence that the changes in terms and conditions are justified, and that it is fair for the company to insist upon them under threat of dismissal. For example, where the company has to relocate and staff representatives accept the change on behalf of junior staff the executive may not be adopting a reasonable position if he continues objecting to the change.

Confidential information

In *Skyrail Oceanic Ltd t/a Goodmos Tours* v *Coleman* [1980] IRLR 226, an employee in the travel agency was dismissed because she was about to marry an employee in a rival firm. The two firms had consulted each other and agreed on this action on the basis that, although both were booking clerks and had no financial interest in their companies, the dismissed employee did have access to confidential information. The EAT accepted that in principle the dismissal could be justified under the heading "some other substantial reason".

Other fair dismissals

Apart from protection of business interests, a number of other cases illustrate the potential scope of the category of "some other substantial reason".

Temporary engagements

Where an executive has been taken on under a temporary contract and it has been made clear to him that the contract is of this nature, the company's refusal to renew it is likely to constitute a fair dismissal being for a substantial reason.

Personality differences

In *Treganowan* v *Robert Knee & Co Ltd* [1975] IRLR 247, Ms Treganowan worked in an office with other women. The atmosphere in the office had become so tense that it was unbearable and was seriously affecting the company's business. The cause of the trouble was a personality clash between T and the other employees for which T was to blame. Apparently the hostility arose "from a difference of opinion as to the merits of the permissive society" and T was "completely insensitive to the atmosphere". She already had an illegitimate child and now she was boasting of her association with a man almost half her age. The Truro tribunal held that this constituted "some other substantial reason" and that the dismissal was not unfair.

In the context of senior employment, it is conceivable that clashes of personality among board members may necessitate the removal of a director, so that the company can be managed effectively (one of the principal aims of the recent Combined Code on Corporate Governance). Provided the company acts reasonably, this could potentially amount to a substantial reason justifying dismissal.

Dismissal at behest of third parties

Exceptionally a company may be requested or required to dismiss an executive by a third party. In these circumstances the dismissal may be fair even though the company is reluctant to dismiss and does not agree with the decision. For example, if an executive upsets a major customer who then insists on his dismissal, this may be fair. However, as the EAT made clear in *Grootcon (UK) Ltd* v *Keld* [1984] IRLR 302, if the company wishes to rely upon the defence it must prove the case. In that case the employer alleged that they had dismissed an employee who worked on their oil rig at the behest of BP, but failed to indicate how the instruction was given or what consultations there had been with BP prior to dismissal. The company therefore lost the case.

Imprisonment

Where the period of imprisonment prevents the executive performing his duties, the contract of employment may be "frustrated" and both parties would be released from their obligations under it. Imprisonment, of whatever duration, may also justify dismissal although the nature of the offence and length of the sentence will be relevant when the tribunal determines the reasonableness of the company's approach.

Breakdown of trust and confidence

In a suitable case the company may rely upon the breakdown in trust and confidence as a substantial reason justifying the dismissal. However, it must be the act of the executive himself which leads to that breakdown, and not the act of the company or a third party. Where, for example, the executive has consistently abused customer perks or failed to notify the board of an issue of commercial importance to the company, the trust between the parties may be undermined fundamentally, justifying dismissal.

The requirement to act reasonably applies in all the circumstances outlined above. Reasonableness is considered further below at 2.4.

2.3 Constructive dismissal

Having considered the grounds upon which the company may dismiss an executive, remember that a dismissal may also arise where the executive resigns in response to the company's conduct. This is known as a constructive dismissal.

Elements

In order for the executive to be able to claim constructive dismissal, four conditions must be met:

(1) There must be a breach of contract by the company. This may be either an actual breach or an anticipatory breach.
(2) That breach must be sufficiently important to justify the executive resigning ("repudiatory breach"), or else it must be the last in a series of incidents which justify his leaving.
(3) He must leave in response to the breach and not for some other, unconnected reason.
(4) He must not delay too long in terminating the contract in response to the company's breach, otherwise he may be deemed to have waived the breach and agreed to vary the contract.

If the executive leaves in circumstances where these conditions are not met, he will be held to have resigned and there will be no dismissal within the meaning of the legislation at all. These elements are considered below.

Breach of contact

In *Western Excavating (ECC) Ltd v Sharp* [1978] IRLR 27, CA, Mr Sharp requested three hours off one afternoon and, when this was refused, he nevertheless left his work. The next day he was dismissed but a disciplinary panel substituted five days' suspension without pay. Mr Sharp was in financial difficulties and, after he had been refused an advance on his accrued holiday pay and had unsuccessfully requested a loan of £40 from his employers, he resigned in order to obtain his holiday pay. The Court of Appeal made it clear that questions of constructive dismissal should be determined according to the terms of the contractual relationship and not in accordance with a test of "reasonable conduct by the company". The company may not have acted reasonably but had not acted in breach of contract and Mr Sharp had not been dismissed.

Lord Denning summarised the differences between the contract and reasonableness tests before concluding that the former should apply. An important reason for this was that the test of unreasonable conduct was too indefinite by far and had led to findings of constructive dismissal on the most whimsical grounds. The contract test was, he thought, more certain and could be understood by intelligent laymen under the direction of a legal chairman.

What is a breach of contract?

Obviously this depends upon the particular circumstances of the case, though it is important to emphasise that in determining the contractual terms, employment tribunals must apply principles of law in the ordinary way and are not entitled to apply different or more lax principles merely because the case is set in an industrial context. For example, if the company unilaterally reduces the pay of the executive or unilaterally changes his job duties or insists upon him working hours which he is not contractually obliged to work, the executive may leave and claim constructive dismissal.

It follows that the company's actions will not constitute a breach of contract if the express terms of the executive's contract permit the contract to be varied in the particular manner adopted. In executive contracts, for example, it is common for duties clauses to be fairly widely drafted with an obligation on the executive to perform "such duties as may be assigned to him by the board from time to time".

Implied duty of trust and confidence

Employment contracts contain certain implied terms, one of which is the duty of mutual trust and confidence. Breach of this term by an employer can lead to constructive dismissal. This was the case in *Mahmud v Bank of Credit and Commerce International SA* [1997] ICR 606, where the House of Lords held that:

> "The company shall not without reasonable and proper cause conduct itself in a manner calculated and likely to destroy or seriously damage the relationship of confidence and trust between employer and employee."

In *Mahmud* itself the relevant breach was the dishonest and corrupt running of a business by the company. This, held the court, was capable of involving a breach of the term even though the individual executive may not personally be required to become involved in criminal activity.

Their Lordships held that this term may be broken even in circumstances where the executive actually remains indifferent to the conduct in issue. It is enough that, viewed objectively, the conduct is likely to destroy or seriously damage the trust and confidence between company and executive.

This term not to undermine trust and confidence is of potentially wide scope. It can extend to extremely inconsiderate or thoughtless behaviour. For example, refusing to investigate complaints promptly and reasonably is capable of falling into this category. Similarly, unacceptable abuse may fall within its scope and indeed any conduct which is "so intolerable that it amounts to a repudiation of the contract".

It is not possible to provide an exhaustive list of conduct which might involve a breach of this duty. However, examples from case law include:

- failing properly to investigate allegations of sexual harassment, or generally to provide the executive with prompt redress of grievances;
- failing to give reasonable support to enable the executive to carry out the duties of his job without disruption or harassment from fellow workers;
- falsely and without reasonable cause accusing an executive of theft;
- undermining the position of a supervisor by upbraiding him in the presence of his subordinates;
- reprimanding in a degrading, intimidating or humiliating manner;
- failing to treat a longserving executive with dignity and consideration;
- persistently attempting to vary an executive's conditions of service;
- making persistent and unwanted amorous advances towards executives; and
- failing to provide a safe and suitable working environment.

Fairness in disciplinary sanctions

In *BBC v Beckett* [1983] IRLR 43 the EAT accepted that it can be a breach of contract for a company to impose a disciplinary sanction which is out of all proportion to the offence. The executive had been downgraded following disciplinary proceedings. Even though the contract of employment explicitly provided that demotion might be imposed for an act of misconduct, the employment tribunal held that it was far too harsh for the particular misconduct and that when Mr Beckett resigned he was entitled to treat himself as having been constructively dismissed.

"Stigma" damages

The courts have recently developed a new head of loss which may arise from a breach of the implied duty of trust and confidence. In *Malik* v *Bank of Credit and Commerce International* [1997] IRLR 462 it was decided that executives could recover stigma damages from their employers. This is compensation for financial loss arising from damage to personal reputation, and such damages potentially extend beyond the notice period to a longer period during which the executive is likely to be precluded from gaining alternative employment (see further Chap 6).

While the facts of the case were fairly unusual, involving the dishonest conduct of business at BCCI, the implications of the case are potentially significant. The court stated:

> "Employers must take care not to damage the executive's future employment prospects by harsh and oppressive behaviour or by any other form of conduct not acceptable today as falling below the standards set by the implied term of mutual trust and confidence."

The manner and circumstances of dismissal could give rise to such a claim. Companies should remember that every employment contract contains the implied term of trust and confidence, and be sensitive to such issues. The relevance of *Malik* to disciplinary procedures is that where an executive is dismissed before he has time to explain, or where there has been insufficient investigation generally, the operation of the procedure will be faulty and the manner of the dismissal will breach the implied term. An inadequate allegation of gross misconduct may taint the executive's reputation and make it very difficult for him to work again. The executive may, in such circumstances, claim "stigma" damages.

Anticipatory breach

Generally the executive will leave in response to an actual breach of contract by the company. However, a constructive dismissal may also arise where the executive leaves in response to an anticipatory breach, *i.e.* a situation where the company indicates that it is proposing to break the contract at some point in the future.

The mere fact that the company genuinely misunderstands its powers under the contract will not of itself constitute an anticipatory breach.

The executive would not succeed in claiming resignation in response to anticipatory breach where the company has not yet taken up an entrenched position.

Resignation in response

The executive must leave in response to the breach which may be actual or anticipatory. Where there has been no breach by the company prior to resignation, the company's conduct subsequently will not convert that resignation into a constructive dismissal. So, when an executive who thought she was suspected of theft resigned, and was subsequently refused her wages unless she confirmed her resignation in writing, the offending action of the company did not result in her being dismissed. The company's conduct was subsequent to the resignation and irrelevant to the question of constructive dismissal.

Waiving the breach

In the *Western Excavating* case [1978] QB 761 Lord Denning commented that the executive:

> "must make up his mind soon after the conduct of which he complains; for, if he continues for any length of time without leaving, he will lose his right to treat himself as discharged."

In these circumstances the executive will be deemed to have agreed the new arrangements (*i.e.* waived the breach). Where, for example, the company imposes a unilateral reduction in wages the executive may be treated as having agreed to the variation if he accepts the lower wages. Thereafter the conduct of the company would not constitute a breach.

There is no fixed time within which the executive must make up his mind. It depends upon all the circumstances including his length of service, the nature of the breach, and whether the executive has protested at the change.

Where the executive is faced with giving up his job and being unemployed or waiving the breach, it is not surprising that the courts are reluctant to conclude that he has lost his right to treat himself as discharged by the company merely by contributing to work in the job for a few months.

Resignations not constituting constructive dismissal

If the executive leaves and does not meet the four conditions outlined above, there will be no dismissal for the purpose of the legislation. Indeed, unless the executive gives the notice he is required to give under his contract, the resignation will be in breach of contract.

Moreover, the executive who resigns in this way will not in general, without the agreement of the company, be entitled to withdraw his resignation.

2.4 **Reasonableness**

Apart from those cases where a dismissal is automatically unfair, establishing a fair reason for dismissal is only the first stage in defending an unfair dismissal claim. In addition, under section 98(4) of the Employment Rights Act 1996 the tribunal must be satisfied that the company has acted reasonably in all the circumstances. Companies often decide before initiating a procedure that the executive must go. The procedure will then be undertaken for form's sake in the hope of avoiding an unfair dismissal claim. The underlying principle of following a fair procedure is to retain employees. If it is undertaken with the outcome already having been decided, it will be a sham and unfair.

The statutory test of fairness is as follows:

> " ... the determination of the question whether the dismissal was fair or unfair, having regard to the reason shown by the company:
> (a) depends on whether in the circumstances (including the size and administrative resources of the company's undertaking) the company acted reasonably or unreasonably in treating it as a sufficient reason for dismissing the executive, and
> (b) shall be determined in accordance with equity and the substantial merits of the case."

The statutory requirement is therefore very general. In practice, certain guidelines or principles have been established dealing with commonly recurring areas of dismissal, such as misconduct, capability and redundancy. Failure to meet the standards reflected in these principles does not render a dismissal automatically unfair, but these principles indicate the sort of conduct which a tribunal will generally expect of a company handling an executive severance.

How does it work in practice?

The one clear principle is that it is not for the tribunal simply to substitute its own opinion for that of the company as to whether certain conduct is reasonable or not. Its job is to determine whether the company has acted in a manner in which a reasonable employer might have acted, even though the tribunal, left to itself, would have acted differently.

The tribunal recognises that in many (though not all) cases there is a band of reasonable responses to the executive's conduct within which individual companies might reasonably take differing views.

Therefore, in looking at whether dismissal was an appropriate sanction, the question is not whether some lesser sanction would, in the company's view, have been appropriate, but rather whether dismissal was within the band of reasonable responses that a company could reasonably make in the circumstances.

Factors which must be considered

There are two factors which must, where relevant, be taken into account by a tribunal when determining whether or not a company has acted reasonably.

Size and administrative resources of the company

This factor will be relevant in a wide range of situations. In *Bevan Harris Ltd* v *Gair* [1981] IRLR 520, the EAT thought it particularly relevant where the issue under consideration was whether alternative employment should have been offered to a man dismissed for incompetence. In a small firm there was no need for an elaborate disciplinary or appeals procedure. The close personal ties between the company and employees would generally render such formalities unnecessary.

But certain matters cannot be explained or justified on the grounds that the company is a small company. In *Henderson* v *Granville Tours Ltd* [1982] IRLR 494 the EAT refused to accept that the size of the undertaking could excuse a failure by the company properly to investigate a complaint made against Mr Henderson, which complaint led to his dismissal.

Codes of Practice

Any relevant Code of Practice must be taken into consideration by a tribunal. In practice the most relevant requirements are those set out in the ACAS Code on Disciplinary Practices and Procedures in Employment. A revised Code of Practice came into effect on 5 February 1998. This emphasises in particular the key procedural safeguards which should ideally apply to disciplinary cases, namely a warning procedure, a chance to state a case and a right of appeal. These elements are essential to a fair dismissal on grounds of conduct or capability. In the context of executive severance, procedures have tended historically to be applied more haphazardly (if at all) than is the case of less senior employees. This is particularly the case where the company takes the view that whether or not a fair procedure is followed, there will be no difference to the outcome, namely dismissal.

Can a dismissal be unfair because of procedural failings in circumstances where the executive would have been dismissed in any event?

In *Polkey* v *A E Dayton Services Ltd* [1987] 3 All ER 974, Lord Bridge set down principles which strongly emphasised the importance of procedural safeguards and which still guide employers today.

> "Employers contesting a claim of unfair dismissal will commonly advance as their reason for dismissal one of the reasons specifically recognised as valid by [s 98(2) of the ERA]. These, put shortly, are: (a) that the employee could not do his job properly; (b) that he had been guilty of misconduct; (c) that he was redundant. But an employer having prima facie grounds to dismiss for one of these reasons will in the great majority of cases not act reasonably in treating the reason as a sufficient reason for dismissal unless and until he has taken the steps, conveniently classified in most of the authorities as procedural, which are necessary in the circumstances of the case to justify that course of action. Thus, in the case of incapacity, the employer will normally not act reasonably unless he gives the employee fair warning and an opportunity to mend his ways and show that he can do the job; in the case of misconduct, the employer will normally not act reasonably unless he investigates the complaint of misconduct fully and fairly and hears whatever the employee wishes to say in his defence or in explanation or mitigation; in the case of redundancy, the employer will normally not act reasonably unless he warns and consults any employees affected or their representative, adopts a fair basis on which to select for redundancy and takes such steps as may be reasonable to avoid or minimise redundancy by redeployment within his own organisation. If an employer has failed to take the appropriate procedural steps in any particular case, the one question the industrial tribunal is not permitted to ask in applying the test of reasonableness posed by [s 98(4) ERA] is the hypothetical question whether it would have made any difference to the outcome if the appropriate procedural steps had been taken. On the true construction of [s 98(4)] this question is simply irrelevant. It is quite a different matter if the tribunal is able to conclude that the employer himself, at the time of dismissal, acted reasonably in taking the view that,

in the exceptional circumstances of the particular case, the procedural steps normally appropriate would have been futile, could not have altered the decision to dismiss and therefore could be dispensed with. In such a case the test of reasonableness under [s 98(4)] may be satisfied."

Tribunals therefore should start from the premise that breach of procedures, at least where they embody significant safeguards for the executive, will render a dismissal unfair. It will only very rarely be the case that a failure to give a hearing can be justified: tribunals will not be quick to conclude that a company has acted fairly in dispensing with essential procedural safeguards. This is so even in redundancy cases where the need to dismiss is clear. The executive may, for example, wish to have the opportunity to persuade the company to give him a more junior post, or accept a reduction in salary.

However, as *Polkey* itself makes clear, the question of how the executive would have been treated had a fair procedure been adopted is not wholly irrelevant in unfair dismissal claims. While it is immaterial to the issue of whether the dismissal was fair or not, it will be highly relevant to the question of the appropriate remedy and, in particular, what, if any, compensation should be awarded.

The appeal stage of the disciplinary process is as important in the context of fairness and reasonableness as the initial process itself. If an appeal hearing is sufficiently comprehensive it is capable of remedying earlier defects in the disciplinary process. However, in order to do so the appeal should be in the nature of a full rehearing rather than merely constituting a review of the initial decision.

Other factors

Finally, the company should consider other factors of general application which are sometimes taken into account. Length of service will almost always be a relevant factor.

In misconduct cases it may influence the question whether dismissal is a fair sanction to impose, and it may lead a tribunal to take the view that a reasonable company ought to give the benefit of the doubt to long serving executives where evidence is in conflict. Length of service is particularly relevant in redundancy cases where redundancy selection is under consideration.

Another factor relevant to the concept of reasonableness is consistency. Inconsistent behaviour by the company may render the dismissal unfair.

Generally the inconsistent behaviour will arise in one of two ways:

- the company may treat executives in a similar position differently;
- it may in relation to a particular executive have treated certain conduct leniently in the past and then suddenly treat it as a dismissible offence without any warning of this change in attitude.

Both forms of inconsistency may render a dismissal unfair.

A company is entitled to take into account not only the nature of the conduct and the surrounding facts but also any mitigating personal circumstances affecting the executive concerned. The attitude of the executive to his conduct may be a relevant factor in deciding whether a repetition is likely. Thus an executive who admits that his conduct is unacceptable and accepts advice and help to avoid a repetition may be regarded differently from one who refuses to accept responsibility for his actions, argues with the board or makes unfounded suggestions that others have conspired to accuse him falsely.

Events occurring after notice of dismissal

Where dismissal is with notice, the test of fairness is not simply applied to the facts as they existed at the date notice was given. Events which occur during the notice period, or which emerge in the appeal process may have an impact on whether or not the company has acted reasonably in all the circumstances.

2.5 **Discrimination**

Where an executive termination has been mishandled, the executive's lawyer may include allegations of discrimination in order to increase pressure on the company to make a speedy and generous settlement. This can be a powerful tactical move. Allegations of discrimination can be extremely difficult to defend because the tribunal is entitled to draw inferences of discrimination from any unusual, or improper conduct on the part of the company in recognition of the fact that incidents of overt discrimination are increasingly rare. Since discrimination operates at a more subtle (even subconscious) level, tribunals are alert to the possibility of discrimination being a factor in the decision to terminate employment.

Discrimination in the context of executive termination may either be direct or indirect.

- **direct**   the individual suffers less favourable treatment to his detriment on the grounds of sex, race or disability;
- **indirect**   the company imposes a requirement on the work force with which a woman (or a man), or a person of a particular race, cannot comply where the proportion of women, or people of that race, who can comply with the requirement is *considerably smaller* than the proportion of men, or people of another race, who can comply.

A third type of discrimination is **victimisation**. An executive is "victimised" under the discrimination legislation where he suffers detrimental treatment as a result of asserting a right under the discrimination legislation, or assisting another in doing so.

Where an executive has been discriminated against he may bring a claim at the employment tribunal. Compensation is not subject to a statutory maximum (unlike unfair dismissal compensation), and there may also be an award for injury to feeling (see also Chap 6). The employment tribunal also has power to make recommendations to the company in order to prevent subsequent incidents of discrimination. These could obviously cause the company considerable embarrassment and cost, and may invite the attentions of the Equal Opportunities Commission or Commission for Racial Equality. It should also be remembered that both the company and individual executives/ directors can be held liable for discrimination under the relevant acts. Executives' representatives may, therefore, cite senior executives as second respondents in employment tribunal proceedings, again in an attempt to embarrass the company into a quick settlement.

Direct discrimination

Companies may be vulnerable to discrimination claims because of the nature of an executive severance. The reason for an executive being asked to leave a company may not easily be identified, because it is to do with commercial considerations which may not be familiar to employment tribunals. The allegation that "his face didn't fit" is potentially very dangerous because it is highly subjective and the tribunal would be likely to consider that it admits the possibility of discrimination (*King* v *Great Britain – China Centre* [1991] IRLR 513).

The company must, therefore, have sound objective business reasons for the termination in order to be able to justify the decision before a tribunal.

Indirect discrimination

Recent surveys demonstrate that there are still very few women in senior positions in industry. It is still the case that more women than men have primary child caring responsibility and the hours of work for senior executives are often inconsistent with family life. Companies should be sensitive to the fact that senior female executives may not be able to comply with travel or working hours requirements imposed upon them by the company. Where such requirements cannot be justified on objective grounds, a claim of indirect discrimination could succeed. Family friendly employment laws (such as parental leave, flexible working, etc) will provide further areas of potential indirect discrimination. Working practices that prevent female executives exercising their family friendly rights may expose employers to costly claims. Where the company is heavy-handed about such matters it is also possible that the executive concerned may claim constructive dismissal, on the basis that the company was breaching the implied duty of trust and confidence.

Key points for dismissal

Have you got grounds?

- redundancy
- capability
- conduct
- illegality
- SOSR

Can you dismiss without notice or pay in lieu of notice?

- fundamental breach of contract
  e.g. performance/conduct (breach of fiduciary duties/statutory duties under the Companies Act 1985)

Be reasonable

- procedural safeguards
- length of executive's service
- consistency
- range of reasonable responses
- tribunal will not substitute its own view

Other issues

- protection of business interests (see Chap 7)
- damage to the executive's reputation
- is the disciplinary procedure contractual?

Chapter 3

· Preparations for Dismissal ·

3.1 What do you want?

Having established whether there are grounds for the company to terminate the executive's employment, before commencing the process of termination it is important to take stock of what the company is trying to achieve.

Depending on the executive's position at the company and the different offices and/or interests he may hold, it may be important not only to ensure effective termination of employment, but also to end directorships and trusteeships and to acquire any shares the executive may hold. In each case, it is vital to consider any documentation governing the relationship to ensure that the relationship is terminated properly in accordance with written procedures or agreements.

The main issue in almost every case will be the effective termination of employment and preparing for dismissal by considering the terms of the employment contract (see further below). However, where the executive wears hats in addition to his employee hat (for example, he is a director or shareholder) what issues arise?

3.2 Is the executive a director?

If so, it will be important that his role as an officer of the company ends at the same time as the executive's employment.

Effecting termination of the directorship

Where the severance is amicable, the executive will usually be prepared to resign his directorships within the company or, where relevant, group companies. Even if it is not an amicable departure, the executive may not wish to continue as a director once employment ends. As director, the executive will have duties and liabilities which will exist as long as he remains a director, even if he is no longer an employee. Most directors will not wish to continue with those liabilities after the termination of their employment contract, and can be persuaded to resign their directorships. Where the executive does not resign his office however, or where he is being forced out, the company will need to consider what powers it has to end the office. The company may have one or more of the following options:

- removal under the executive's employment contract;
- removal under the Articles of Association;
- removal by shareholders;
- removal by the board of directors;

Removal under executive's employment contract

The most straightforward method, provided it is available to the company, is to terminate the directorship under the terms of the executive's employment contract. The company should therefore check the employment contract to see whether it contains a requirement for the executive to resign as a director if his employment comes to an end. The company should also check whether any such requirement kicks in if employment ends for any reason, or if it is limited to the employment ending for specific reasons. Often the requirement is supplemented in the employment contract by a power of attorney so that if the executive refuses to comply with the terms of his employment contract and resign his directorships, there is a power for a nominee of the company to resign on his behalf and to complete the appropriate documentation (including filing forms at Companies House). Commentators have questioned whether such a power would be effective in practice.

Conversely, it may be that in certain cases an executive ceases to be a director but remains an employee. The directorship may end through the executive's own choice or because the executive is not eligible to continue as a director (for example, because of bankruptcy). Where a company no longer wishes to employ an executive who cannot or will not continue as a director, again the company should look to the terms of the employment contract to check whether there is any provision entitling the company to terminate the employment relationship instantly.

Removal under Articles of Association

There is provision in standard Table A Articles for the automatic disqualification and removal of a director in specific circumstances. These circumstances are as follows:

- ceasing to be a director pursuant to the Companies Act or becoming prohibited by law from being a director;
- becoming bankrupt or making any arrangement/composition with creditors;
- being seriously incapable through mental illness;
- being absent from board meetings for more than six consecutive months.

Where there is no automatic provision within the Articles of Association for ending the directorship and there is no provision in the employment contract requiring the executive to resign his directorship, it will be necessary to turn to the shareholders or where they are properly empowered by the shareholders, the board of directors, to effect dismissal.

Removal by shareholders

Shareholders may remove a director from office at any time by following a procedure set out in section 303 of the Companies Act 1985. The disadvantage of having to remove a director from office by this means is the fact that there is a specified procedure which must be followed and the procedure takes time. However, where it is necessary, the essential features of the procedure are:

- special notice from those shareholders who wish to try to remove a director to the company of their resolution to so remove him (to be sent to the company's registered office 28 days before the general meeting when removal will be considered);
- holding a general meeting (for which appropriate notice must be given to all shareholders);
- notice of the proposed resolution to remove the director must also be given to the director concerned;
- the director may make representations (both oral and written);
- at the general meeting, the resolution to remove the director will be passed if a simple majority vote in favour of it.

Note that it will not be necessary to resort to the section 303 of the Companies Act procedure where *all* of the shareholders unanimously agree to remove a director.

Removal by board of directors

The board of directors may pass a resolution approving the removal of one of their number. Such a resolution would be passed by a simple majority of the directors. This is quite a straightforward route, but it is vital that in passing such a resolution the directors have the shareholders' unanimous support. This is so that the directors' resolution can stand as an act of the company, (*i.e.* something which is approved by all of the shareholders). A directors' resolution which can be unanimously approved by the shareholders, is likely only to be of use in smaller private companies where the directors (with the exception of the director it is proposed to remove) are also shareholders. Clearly, if the director who is earmarked for removal is also a shareholder, it is highly unlikely that there would be *unanimous* shareholder approval for the directors' resolution.

3.3 **Is the executive a shareholder?**

Where the executive owns shares in the company, the company must consider whether or not the size of the shareholding is such that the executive should sell his shares back to the company.

In many cases the company may want a global settlement whereby the relationship with the executive is severed once and for all including divesting the executive of any shares he may hold. This may not be appropriate or necessary where the company is listed and there is an open market for the shares. It may, however, be a very important issue in the case of individuals who were directors or senior executives in small private or family companies. A shareholding of 25% or more would enable an executive who has been dismissed to continue to wield considerable power in respect of the management of the company as the individual would be able to block ordinary resolutions. Commonly, in such cases, the company's Articles of Association would provide for the executive to sell his shares to the company in the event of termination of employment. If, however, there is no such provision, the individual's shareholding may become an important part of the severance negotiations. Ultimately it will become a negotiation over price and circumstances will dictate how demanding the executive can be in this regard.

Even executives with relatively minor shareholdings may cause difficulties for their former employer.. Executives with shareholdings of at least 10% of the issued shares are entitled to call an extraordinary general meeting, whilst individuals holding 5% of the issued shares are entitled to have an item placed on the agenda for the annual general meeting. As a minority shareholder, the executive has minority shareholder rights, including the right to have the company wound up on the ground that it is just and equitable to do so and under section 459 of the Companies Act 1985 the right to petition the court if he has no executive power having been dismissed as an employee/director and feels that he is being unfairly prejudiced by what is happening within the company.

3.4 Impact of contract on termination as an employee

Chapter 2 looked at the possible reasons for termination and the requirements for a termination to be lawful and Chapter 4 will consider how commercial and other considerations interact with the strict legal requirements for a fair and lawful dismissal. However, before doing so, an important issue is to get to grips with how the employment documentation will affect the dismissal. In other words, in the particular circumstances of the proposed dismissal, do certain clauses or provisions in the individual's contract help either the executive or the company?

Accordingly, prior to dismissing the executive, the company should review the relevant employment documentation including, in particular, the employment contract, but also the employment handbook, where there is one, and any other relevant documents, for example, pension scheme rules, bonus scheme rules.

Most executives' employment contracts contain certain standard clauses (tailored of course to suit the particular company). Where these clauses are useful to the company but absent from the employment contract, it may be possible to include them in a negotiated severance agreement provided the financial incentive for the executive to agree to them is sufficient. Some of the standard contractual clauses are set out below, together with an outline of their effect. The operation and effect of such clauses may have a significant impact on the way a termination is effected.

3.5 **Sample Clauses**

Sample Clauses	Effect
■ Pay in lieu of notice *The company reserves the right to terminate this agreement immediately without giving you notice by paying to you your contractual remuneration (less deductions for tax and national insurance) in lieu of all or part of the notice period.*	■ Company may lawfully terminate contract immediately whether or not there are grounds for instant dismissal; ■ Company must pay in lieu - but does the employment contract limit this to salary (as is recommended) or refer to total contractual remuneration (will this include bonus?). If so, how will the value of bonus and benefits be calculated? ■ If post-termination restrictions are important, ensure the employment contract is ended lawfully whether by notice or payment in lieu of notice. This is because a termination in breach of contract will deprive the company of the benefit of the restrictions (see Chap 7). ■ Ideally, if there is a long notice period, your contractual clause (either in the employment contract or the negotiated severance agreement) will provide for instalment payments which will continue only until the executive obtains another job. ■ Payments made under a clause such as this cannot benefit from the £30,000 tax exemption (see Chap 6).

Sample Clauses	Effect
■ Bonus *You are entitled to participate in the company s bonus scheme and to receive such bonus as the company may in its absolute discretion determine provided you are in employment with the company and not under notice or subject to the company s disciplinary procedure on the payment date.*	■ There is a contractual entitlement to participate in a bonus scheme; ■ There is an onus on the company not to exercise its discretion in relation to awarding bonus capriciously; ■ If the executive is paid in lieu of notice, payment in lieu may have to take account of a sum for bonus if the payment in lieu clause is not limited to salary; ■ The proviso would enable the company to argue that there is no contractual entitlement to bonus where employment has ended, or the executive is under notice or being disciplined when bonus would normally be paid.
■ Garden leave ■ *Where either you or the company has given the other notice of termination or you resign whether with or without notice, provided you continue to receive your full contractual benefits until your employment terminates, the company may for all or part of your notice period:* ■ *exclude you from company premises;* ■ *require you to carry out different or no duties;* ■ *instruct you not to contact or communicate orally or in writing with clients, suppliers or employees of the company.*	■ Allows the company to put the executive in the garden so giving the company protection for its business during the notice period; ■ the executive must continue to receive his whole remuneration during the notice period; ■ the executive is still employed as garden leave operates during the notice period. As such the executive continues to owe all fiduciary and loyalty duties to the company; ■ but, an executive whose job or skills require him to be actively working in order to maintain those skills may not be able to be placed on garden leave (see Chap 7).

Sample Clauses	Effect
■ Disciplinary procedure Either *The Company's disciplinary procedure is set out as Schedule 1 to the agreement.* or *The Company has a disciplinary procedure which is set out in the Handbook. The disciplinary procedure does not form part of your contract of employment.* or *The Company does not have a disciplinary procedure which is applicable to you.*	■ The first example incorporates the procedure into the contract. Thus there is a procedure to follow (best practice for unfair dismissal) but a failure to follow it will mean a breach of contract. ■ The second example is an improvement as the disciplinary procedure is expressly excluded from the contract. ■ The third example will not necessarily absolve the company in terms of an unfair dismissal claim. In the light of the duty to act reasonably in relation to disciplinary matters, it is preferable to have some sort of procedure which is applicable to all employees, including executives. However, the procedure may be truncated for executives (as a reflection of their seniority) and to shorten the time involved.

Chapter 4

How Are We Getting There?

4.1 Introduction

Each executive severance will be different. The aim of this chapter is to highlight some of the miscellaneous practical concerns which arise before, during and after an executive termination.

4.2 Strategy

It is in the interests of the company that executive severances should be planned so that "a clean break" is effected. The company will have to take a view on how it intends to effect the termination, bearing in mind any commercial requirements and the need to protect its business. The options available to the company will be driven very much by the facts of each case, but they will broadly fall into the following:

- dismiss immediately with or without a payment in lieu of notice and wait for litigation - then fight or negotiate a settlement;
- dismiss immediately with or without a payment in lieu (again note the "fighting fund" issue)and negotiate;
- negotiate a settlement before giving notice of termination, (although a payment in lieu may provide the executive with "a fighting fund" to bring claims);
- give notice of termination according to the employment contract (deciding whether to put the executive on garden leave during the notice period) and negotiate a severance package during the notice period.

"Best practice" dismissal

Chapter 2 of this book highlights the possible grounds for terminating employment taking into account the terms of the employment contract and the issue of fairness in the context of statutory rights. From a contractual perspective, the most effective dismissal (in terms of costs and the avoidance of litigation and assuming there are no grounds allowing for instant dismissal) will be where the executive receives notice or pay in lieu of notice and any contractual disciplinary procedure is followed.

In the statutory context, depending on the circumstances, it may be that the company needs to conduct a full investigation and follow a procedure before termination in order to be able to demonstrate fairness.

Frequently, there will be commercial or other considerations which mean that the "best practice" dismissal will not be appropriate or possible. Where, for example, a valued customer indicates that it will discontinue doing business with the company if the executive remains on the account, would the company be able to afford the time to follow a disciplinary procedure, particularly when to do so would serve no practical purpose in terms of improving relations between the executive and the customer? In such circumstances, the company will have to adjust its position and prepare a strategy which takes account of the company's objectives, its resources, the time available, the precedents which it wishes to set and the executive's contractual and statutory rights. Occasionally, the decision as to which strategy to adopt will have been taken out of the hands of the company due to the fact that the executive has already been dismissed or has resigned (perhaps following closed door discussions with a senior colleague) in which case the company's room for manoeuvre will be limited.

4.3 Negotiations and other issues

Costs and resources

This is likely to be one of the most important areas for the company. Has it calculated the costs involved in the termination and if so can that money be made available immediately? Costs are likely to include payment in lieu of notice or damages for loss of office, compensation for loss of benefits, pension contributions, possible buy-out of the executive's shareholding and a contribution towards his legal fees. In addition, the company may have to make provision for its own legal costs and be aware that further costs may arise, particularly if the matter becomes contentious. Costing the deal has been addressed in detail in Chapter 6.

Precedent

Is the company establishing a precedent in the terms of settlement which other executives may claim in the future? This is especially relevant where the company is facing the departure of a number of executives or a team of executives. Note that reference to previous severance deals will also add weight to an argument that custom and practice has effectively established an implied right to similar terms. This may especially be so in a redundancy where enhanced terms have been made available to senior employees. Employees affected by subsequent redundancy exercises may claim an implied contractual entitlement to the same enhanced terms.

Negotiating space

The company will not, of course, want to invite or become embroiled in litigation given its objective to achieve a "commercial" outcome. Indeed, it will be a primary aim of management and the HR team to avoid litigation. Instead, the company will want to create some space to negotiate with the executive. This will be particularly important where the company has got its procedures wrong or does not wish to go through a prolonged internal procedure. However, in entering into settlement negotiations, the company will not want to weaken its position in the event that settlement is not possible and litigation seems inevitable.

Trying to achieve settlement through negotiation whilst at the same time maintaining a strong line justifying the company's action in terminating employment involves two positions being run in parallel:

- the "on the record" defence position; and
- the "without prejudice" negotiating position.

Often the reason why these approaches are adopted concurrently is because the employer appreciates that it may not have sufficient evidence to support the reason for termination of the executive's employment, or that the reasons given for and the procedure leading up to termination would not stand up to close scrutiny in the context of the executive's legal claims. Accordingly, the company tries to do a deal with the executive with a view to achieving its commercial aim of a swift, clean and cost effective break whilst at the same time making it not worth the executive's while to pursue his potential legal claims.

The advantage to the company of adopting simultaneously an "on the record" position and a "without prejudice" negotiating stance is that it can maintain a robust line supporting its reasons for dismissal and arguing against the executive's claims whilst exploring settlement possibilities. This is possible because whilst "on the record" correspondence, documents and discussions may be referred to in evidence before the court in any subsequent legal proceedings, "without prejudice" exchanges cannot be brought to the court's attention subsequently except where the parties involved agree to waive the "without prejudice" qualification. The "without prejudice" qualification enables the parties to continue negotiations towards a settlement both before legal proceedings have been issued and also after proceedings are underway. Note that even in "without prejudice" discussions the company does not have to, nor should it, admit liability.

Another advantage to a "without prejudice" dialogue is that it may be possible for the company and the executive to achieve an amicable settlement which then enables them to maintain a future business relationship.

Negotiating tactics

Tactics will usually depend on varying factors in each instance, including the strength of the case for dismissal, whether or not dismissal has already taken place, whether negotiations are amicable or not, and the amount of money which is available for a deal. There are also different methods and styles of negotiation. There are, however, some key points to consider and various tactical approaches to making an offer of settlement:

"Without prejudice subject to costs"

This is a device which reserves to the person using it the right to waive the "without prejudice" qualification of a document or letter if the question of costs comes to be considered at a later date by a court or tribunal. It is commonly used by solicitors, in a "*Calderbank* letter", where the solicitor makes what he considers to be an offer which cannot be beaten by an award made by the court or tribunal or is otherwise reasonable bearing in mind the risks of litigation. By reserving the right to refer to the letter in subsequent proceedings, the tactic carries with it the implicit threat that if the other side continues to prevaricate or litigate, the court may make an award of costs against them, or they will face an application in a tribunal that they have conducted their case unreasonably or vexatiously.

"Subject to contract"

The words "subject to contract" place all negotiations under the premise that none of the terms which have been agreed individually will bind the parties until the entire severance agreement has been finalised. In the employment context, the use of the qualification ensures that even if the figures of the severance payment are agreed, neither party is bound until all the details of the severance – including the terms of any reference, any post-dismissal statement and restrictive covenants – are concluded and agreed.

The "on the record" offer

The company may make an "on the record" offer to settle. Such an offer could be referred to in evidence in any subsequent legal proceedings without the relevant parties having to waive the "without prejudice" qualification.

The "on the record" offer has tactical advantages in certain situations. If, for example, a company believes it has an unanswerable case, it may be tempted to make an "on the record" offer of everything to which the executive is entitled under his contract and in relation to any possible statutory claims. There would, therefore, be no point in the executive litigating and, if he chose to do so, he may be making himself vulnerable to being liable for the company's costs of defending the claims.

The "Part 36" offer

The Part 36 offer is a new tactic introduced under the new Civil Procedure Rules (CPR). The CPR (which took effect in April 1999) are new rules governing High Court and county court actions; they do not apply to the employment tribunals. They were introduced following proposals for reform made by Lord Woolf (see Chap 1). Under the CPR both executives and employers can make a formal offer of settlement in a wrongful dismissal/breach of contract situation, both before and after proceedings have commenced. Tactically, they are useful in that the recipient of such an offer is put under pressure as the recipient becomes liable in relation to the legal fees of the party making the offer. Provided that the Part 36 offer complies with the form set out in the CPR, draconian cost consequences can apply against the party, particularly defendant companies, that refuses to accept the offer and then fails to beat it in a court hearing. This kind of offer may be an attractive tactic for the executive to use against his former employer.

The Part 36 offer is also open to the company. If the executive does not accept such an offer and fails to beat it at trial, he will be liable for the company's costs incurred after the time limit for acceptance has passed – usually 21 days after the offer was received.

Cutting the cake to achieve a deal

The company need not look upon negotiations as an admission of weakness or as an "all or nothing" package. There will be a number of elements to any executive's overall severance package which can be used as sweeteners for persuading the executive to accept a settlement. These may include:

- letting the executive keep the company car or IT equipment;
- making lump sum payments to pension schemes;
- maintaining private health or other insurances for an additional period of time after termination (where this is possible);
- extending the exercise period for share options (if possible);
- offering to contribute towards the executive's legal or other professional fees;
- offering outplacement counselling.

Staff morale

Of importance to the company will be the possible impact of the executive's termination on his former colleagues. The sight of the executive leaving – particularly if escorted out of the building – may adversely affect staff morale. To try to counteract the negative effects of the executive's departure it may be advisable for the company to have reasons or a statement prepared which it can then issue to staff. Ideally this should be agreed with the executive or at the very least he should be informed of the proposed announcement to avoid inflaming what may already be a tense situation. The company should also give some thought to what customers will be told about the whereabouts of the executive (if he is placed on garden leave) or the reasons for his departure. There may, in addition be requirements to notify relevant regulatory authorities, make press announcements, and in the case of listed companies, to inform the London Stock Exchange of the director's departure. Staff should be instructed carefully in what they tell customers and third parties external to the company. In the case of both staff announcements and external announcements the company must avoid defamatory statements about the executive.

Who dismisses?

If the executive is not a director for Companies Act purposes, the person who, on behalf of the employer, conducts the interview leading to dismissal or writes to the executive to terminate his employment, must be authorised to act on behalf of the employer. Further, from a practical point of view, it is important to ensure that it is someone of sufficient seniority and stature to deliver the message of dismissal to someone who will be a senior, highly paid employee.

If the executive is a director of the company for the purposes of the Companies Acts he must be removed from office (if he will not agree to resign) by the appropriate procedure (see Chap 3).

Dismissal interview

Where it is proposed to conduct a meeting with the executive, those present representing the company must ensure that what they say is consistent with the company's overall approach. The company can damage its "on the record" and its negotiating position by talking "off message" in a dismissal or other interview with the executive. It may be helpful to prepare a script (or detailed agenda) covering all the relevant points of the proposed severance. Preparing a first draft severance agreement before the meeting takes place is a guide to all the points which should be covered. Also, in the same way as correspondence will be kept distinctly either "on the record" or "without prejudice", as appropriate, so it should be made clear during discussions which issues are considered to be "on the record" and which "without prejudice". This can be achieved by prefacing any "without prejudice" discussions with the words; "I would now like to talk to you on a without prejudice/off the record basis".

At the dismissal interview, the executive should be left in no doubt that his employment is being terminated. Note that verbal notice of termination of employment will not usually be sufficient to bring the employment contract lawfully to an end. Most employment contracts stipulate that written notice is necessary (even in an instant dismissal) – check the employment contract's terms. However, it is important that any verbal notification of dismissal is unambiguous, as merely indicating an intention to dismiss will not be sufficient to terminate the employment relationship. Similarly, advance warning of a dismissal on a future date will not break the employment relationship unless that advance warning is in itself a breach of contract. In such a case, the executive may respond to advance warning by resigning and claiming constructive dismissal, citing the company's intention to dismiss as the repudiatory breach of contract (see Chap 2 in relation to anticipatory breach of contract).

Key points

As part of the preparation to effect dismissal and conduct settlement negotiations bear in mind the following issues:

- make an early assessment of the executive's and the company's case, assessing strengths and weaknesses in both;

- make an early assessment of the likely costs involved (including both the severance package (see Chap 6) and the potential legal costs);

- set aside the time required to prepare for (including paperwork) and effect dismissal as well as negotiating time;

- seize the initiative through early preparation (particularly of paperwork);

- decide whether the settlement offer is to be "without prejudice" or "on the record";

- ensure all discussions (whether "on the record" or "without prejudice") are in line with the company's objectives and the terms of correspondence;

- take any necessary steps to maintain staff morale;

- consider what announcements need to be made to any relevant regulatory bodies, customers or clients, third parties, shareholders, the press and, in the case of listed companies, an announcement to the London Stock Exchange;

- ensure that all points are agreed before moving from "without prejudice" to binding agreement.

Chapter 5

Documenting the Deal: the Severance Agreement

5.1 Introduction

Having considered the practical concerns which may arise and decided upon the approach to effecting the severance, the next step is to prepare the documentation. As mentioned in Chapter 4, the employer will have its "on the record" position (which will at the very least amount to formal notice of termination of employment and may also include setting out the employer's reasons for dismissal). In addition the employer will probably adopt a "without prejudice" (or negotiating) position. The terms of the severance which are negotiated without prejudice between the employer and the executive, once agreed, will need to be set down in writing in some form of severance agreement. The severance agreement, once signed, will be binding on the employer and the executive. It will also lose its without prejudice and subject to contract status which applied whilst negotiations were ongoing.

5.2 Types of severance agreement

There is no single correct way to document the terms of the severance which have been agreed. It is a matter of personal preference as to whether the document is in the form of a letter, a duplicate of which the executive signs to accept the terms, or a formal agreement which is executed by both the executive and the employer (however, please note the position in relation to new post-termination restraints – see below). Of greater significance is to ensure that the agreement is in a form which is appropriate to achieve settlement of the executive's claims, both contractual and, where applicable, statutory. If there are no statutory claims in issue (this is not likely to be the case in the majority of executive severances, particularly with the reduced qualification period and the increased compensation cap) it will be sufficient to enter into a binding written agreement. However, where there are statutory claims in issue the employer will often want the executive to sign a compromise agreement.

5.3 **What is a compromise agreement?**

"Compromise agreement" is a term used to describe a type of agreement under which, provided all of the relevant conditions set out in the Employment Rights Act 1996 (ERA) are satisfied, an employee may sign away his rights to bring certain claims against his employer. Those conditions (in s 203, ERA as amended recently by the Employment Rights (Dispute Resolution) Act 1998 (ERDRA)), are as follows:

(1) the agreement must be in writing;
(2) it must relate to the particular complaint or complaints;
(3 the executive must have received independent advice from a qualified lawyer or other relevant independent adviser (see below);
(4) the adviser must certify that there is in force a contract of insurance or an indemnity provided for members of a profession or professional body covering the risk of a claim by the executive;
(5) the agreement must identify the adviser by name; and
(6) the agreement must state that the conditions regulating compromise agreements are satisfied.

See Appendix C at page 123, in particular Schedule 1 which sets out a form of adviser's certificate.

The relevant independent adviser

In addition to qualified lawyers, ERDRA provided that from 1 August 1998 a relevant independent adviser could also be:

- either an officer, official, employee or member of an independent trade union who has been certified in writing by the union as competent to give the advice and authorised to give advice on behalf of the union; or
- employees or volunteers giving free advice in advice centres who have been certified in writing by the centre as competent to give the advice and authorised to provide advice on behalf of the centre;

Certain people cannot be relevant independent advisers:

- the employer or associated employer of the executive or an employee of the employer or associated employer. This means that members of the company's HR department cannot provide the executive with independent advice;
- trade union or advice centre workers where the employer is the trade union or advice centre.

If the relevant conditions are not satisfied, the compromise agreement will not be a valid waiver of the executive's claims. There are other means of contracting out of statutory employment rights but in general they will not be relevant in an executive severance (with the exception of where the Advisory, Conciliation and Arbitration Service (ACAS)) has been involved – see further below).

A form of compromise agreement is set out in Appendix C at page 123.

What claims may be compromised?

As mentioned above, the compromise agreement is used to settle statutory employment claims. The advantage of the compromise agreement over a straightforward full and final settlement agreement is that it is an effective means of preventing the executive from bringing claims in the employment tribunal. An agreement which does not comply with the conditions listed above, simply stating that in consideration of a sum of money the executive agrees not to bring any claims against his former employer, will not operate to stop the executive bringing a tribunal claim (although the money paid to the executive will be taken into account in determining his loss for the purposes of assessing damages (see Chap 6)).

Compromise agreements can be used to settle a number of different types of dispute (including unfair dismissal, discrimination and unlawful deductions from wages claims). Note that they cannot be used to waive all employment rights. For example, it is not possible to settle claims in relation to collective information and consultation rights in mass redundancy or business transfer situations. However, for the vast majority of statutory claims which are likely to be in issue during an executive severance (and which may lead to substantial damages awards if successful) the compromise agreement will be indispensable.

Does it settle all claims?

There is an issue about whether it is permissible to use the agreement to achieve a global settlement of all statutory claims which can be so compromised (whether or not all of them are in issue). One of the conditions (referred to above) which must be fulfilled for the agreement to be valid is that the agreement must relate to a *particular complaint*. This suggests that a claim must have been already asserted by the executive. However, commonly the executive may not have asserted all possible claims, let alone issued tribunal proceedings, preferring instead to negotiate to achieve a settlement as soon as possible. The company, if it is going to pay a substantial amount of compensation to the executive, will of course want to ensure that it has settled all possible claims, whether or not they have been asserted by the executive.

It is an open question in law as to whether the compromise agreement can be used to settle more than one statutory claim, particularly when the claims have not been asserted by the executive. Notwithstanding the condition that the agreement must refer to the particular complaint, it is arguable that as the executive will take independent advice (usually from a qualified lawyer) on the agreement's terms, he should be aware that by signing he will lose his right to bring the statutory claims set out in the compromise agreement. If there is any question that the executive does not want to settle a particular claim, the time to refer to that claim and carve it out of the settlement terms is before the compromise agreement is signed. Whilst the question remains open, it is preferable to have a global settlement of claims. The settlement wording in paragraph 9 of the compromise agreement set out at Appendix C (p 123) comprises a global settlement of claims or complaints within the employment legislation (para 9.2.1) and then in paragraph 9.2.2 there is the opportunity to set out the particular complaints in issue.

A separate but related important point in relation to achieving a global settlement of the executive's statutory claims is that it is not possible to compromise claims which may arise after settlement from new facts. In the case of *Sawicki* v *Computacenter Ltd* (1998) a race discrimination claim was settled as part of the compromise agreement settlement terms. However, Ms Sawicki was subsequently allowed to bring a race discrimination claim against her former employer. The claim was for victimisation as a result of her former employer refusing to provide a reference for her. The claim was allowed to proceed because it arose from new facts not in issue at the time of settlement.

Contractual claims

Whilst the compromise agreement is an effective means of settling statutory employment claims, it is important that the settlement provisions also operate to settle any claims arising from the executive's contract of employment. The "full and final settlement" wording used in paragraph 9 of the compromise agreement set out at Appendix C (p 123) covers contractual as well as statutory claims. It is common to see express wording in compromise agreements which specifically excludes settlement of any claims the executive may have for personal injuries or for benefits or rights arising under the pension scheme of which the executive is a member. The executive will frequently want such claims expressly excluded so that if there are any such claims arising out of his employment, he will be free to bring them against his former employer. Even if they are not expressly excluded, it is unlikely that a blanket exclusion of all claims arising out of employment would prevent the executive from subsequently bringing a claim for personal injuries or pension rights. However, where such potential claims are known about when the settlement is being negotiated, the employer should ensure that those claims are specifically included in the settlement provisions. For example, where the executive has been complaining of stress and there is the potential for a personal injury claim to arise as a result of this stress, the company should include express wording settling this claim as well as claims arising under the contract of employment and any relevant statutory claims. (In the situation described, a disability discrimination claim would be a potential statutory claim which should be compromised.)

Before looking at what other terms, aside from the settlement provisions, should be included in the compromise agreement, remember that the agreement should be marked "without prejudice" and subject to contract until the negotiations have been concluded (see further Chap 4).

Other terms of the compromise agreement

In brief, in addition to the settlement terms the compromise agreement should cover the following:

- the termination date and payments up to that date;
- the *ex-gratia* payment (and the tax treatment);
- any benefits to be provided;

- resignation of directorships (if any);
- return of company property;
- confidentiality of the agreement;
- any post-termination restrictions;
- statements and references;
- contribution to legal fees (if any);
- assistance with future litigation.

Who are the parties?

Give consideration as to who are the parties to the agreement. In most cases it will be the executive and the company which employs him. However, in a business transfer the agreement may need to be between the executive and the employer *after* the transfer (the transferee) as well as *before* the transfer (the transferor). This is to reflect the fact that on transfer, liability for the executive's claims passes from transferee to transferor.

What is the consideration?

Think about what consideration the company is offering to the executive and what terms it is asking the executive to accept in return. Often the company will be offering a compensatory sum to the executive in exchange for him waiving his potential claims. In such cases the sum will be good consideration for the waiver.

Matters become more complicated where the company wants the executive to enter into post-employment restrictions which were not in the executive's employment contract. The executive should receive consideration for acceptance of the restraints as well as for waiving his claims. If there is no cash consideration for the new restraints consider whether the agreement should be executed by the executive as a deed (note that this is not necessarily a foolproof means of introducing consideration where there is no cash sum involved). In any event, because of the adverse tax implications in terms of securing the £30,000 tax exemption if there is no cash sum specifically identified as consideration for the introduction of post-termination restraints (see further Chap 6), it is common to attribute some money as being in exchange for acceptance of the new restraints.

Position to the termination date

The compromise agreement should refer to the date of termination of employment whether the date has already passed or is a future date. There should also be provision for payment of salary and, where appropriate, accrued holiday pay up to the termination date (less deductions for tax and national insurance in both cases); (see para 1 of Appendix C, p 123).

If there is any bonus or commission due to the executive for the period up to the termination date this should be included.

Ensure that the position in relation to the executive's outstanding expenses or any loans or other debts owed by the executive to the company is dealt with expressly in the agreement. Remember that if the company writes off the executive's loan, a charge to tax will arise.

Termination payment

Give details of the termination payment, describing it in a way that will assist with the application of the £30,000 tax exemption. Note that if there is a pay in lieu of notice clause in the executive's employment contract, any payment in lieu made pursuant to it will be fully taxable (see Chap 6).

Where tax has to be deducted from the termination payment (whether on the whole amount, or just to the extent it exceeds £30,000) it may be useful to specify the amount of the deduction for tax and national insurance. Also consider whether tax should be deducted at basic or higher rate (this relates to the timing of the P45 form – see further Chap 6).

Is the termination payment to be made in one lump sum or in instalments? Instalments may be attractive to the company for a number of reasons, for example:

- where the company wishes to guarantee the executive will comply with certain conditions or behave properly throughout the period of the payments;
- where the company wants to build in some mitigation by providing that the payments will cease or be reduced if the executive finds new employment (see alternative para 2.1 of Appendix C, p 123); or
- where there is a concern that the agreement will not be effective to waive statutory claims, or the company does

not want the executive to take independent advice thus ruling out using a compromise agreement as the form of severance agreement (see compromise agreement conditions listed above).

Where the company does not wish to proceed using a compromise agreement, but wishes to take some steps to try to prevent the executive from issuing statutory employment claims, the company can make the termination payment payable in instalments, timing the payment date so that the majority of the termination payment falls after the expiry of time limits for issuing statutory claims. The promise of the payment following expiry of the time limits may be sufficient incentive for the executive not to bring statutory claims against his former employer. However, this route does not prevent the executive from issuing proceedings in relation to statutory claims and therefore provides no guarantee to the former employer. that such claims will not be filed. Paragraph 2.1 of Appendix C sets out alternatives for payment of the termination payment either in one lump sum or in instalments (to reflect mitigation). If the purpose of paying in instalments is because a compromise agreement is not an attractive option to the employer but the employer wants to provide an incentive for the executive not to bring statutory claims, the following wording may be appropriate:

> "The Termination Payment will be paid to you in two instalments. The Company will pay you within 14 days of receiving your signed duplicate of this agreement the first instalment of £[   ]. The balance of the Termination Payment being £[   ] will be paid to you on [**insert date 3.5 months after Termination Date**] or within seven days afterwards on condition that you have not commenced any proceedings in the Employment Tribunal, High Court, County Court or otherwise against the Company or any Group Company or any of their respective officers, employees or agents."

Remember to set out expressly the tax treatment of the termination payment.

Benefits

Company car

If the executive has a company car, the company must decide what is to happen to it. Is the executive to be permitted to continue using it during any notice period? If so, it is important to specify when it must be returned and that the executive must keep the car in a good and roadworthy condition and not do anything which results in the insurance policy being avoided. Consider also who will bear the costs of maintenance and fuel and bear in mind that tax will be chargeable on the value of this continued benefit. Alternatively, the company may give the car to the executive or sell it to him at an undervalue. If the car is given or sold to the executive, the car's market value should be agreed and tax deducted accordingly.

Health/life insurance

It may be possible for the company to continue existing insurance and/or health benefits for a period after termination, perhaps until the executive obtains alternative employment. The company should check whether the rules of such benefit schemes cover ex-employees and also check taxation of any continued benefit.

Pensions

On the termination of his employment, the company's responsibilities to continue paying into the executive's pension scheme cease. As part of the severance terms the company may agree to make a special contribution into the pension scheme for the executive's benefit. This can reduce tax payable on the settlement but will obviously reduce the amount of cash immediately available to the executive.

Outplacement counselling and legal fees

If the company wants to provide outplacement counselling for the executive the terms should be included in the compromise agreement (see further Chap 6 in relation to tax treatment).

Where the company is asking the executive to sign a compromise agreement (which necessitates the executive taking independent advice, usually from a qualified lawyer) it is common for the company to make a contribution towards the executive's legal fees. Such a contribution will not attract a charge to tax provided certain conditions are met (including that the legal advice relates to termination of employment and the fees are paid direct to the executive's lawyer – see para 2.2 of Appendix C, p 123).

Tax indemnity

To protect the company, the compromise agreement should include an indemnity from the executive in relation to tax and national insurance contributions which have not already been deducted by the company and which relate to the termination payment and any continuing benefits.

Resignation as director

The company should include a requirement for the executive to resign his directorships (see para 3 of Appendix C, p 123 and also Appendix E, p 131 for a sample letter of resignation).

Company property

The executive will almost certainly hold company property at the time of his termination. Even if the executive's employment contract includes an express requirement to return all company property, the compromise agreement should include a requirement for him to return that property listing, if possible, specific items of property (see para 8 of Appendix C, p 123).

Statements and references

It is usually the case that the company will want to include in the compromise agreement an express "no bad mouthing" provision which requires the executive not to make any statements which are critical of the company. It can also be extended to include other companies in a group, where relevant, and officers and employees of the company and group companies – see paragraph 4.2 of Appendix C, page 123. The executive, particularly if very senior, may insist that the provision be made mutual. If the company agrees, ensure that the "company" is defined carefully for this purpose so that the obligation does not extend to all employees of the company; only to officers of the company.

The company and executive should agree on the recipients of announcements about the executive's departure and the terms of the announcements (if possible, annex the agreed terms to the agreement). It is usual to include an express provision in the compromise agreement to the effect that the terms and existence of the agreement must be kept confidential. If there is no such express provision a court will not imply it. It is important to carve out from this blanket confidentiality provision (if it applies to the company as well as the executive) the right to make any agreed announcements, and to take professional advice or comply with any legal obligation.

The departing executive will often want to negotiate an agreed reference as part of the severance package. In agreeing the reference, the company should not include misleading or inaccurate statements. The agreement may provide that the executive will receive the reference on the company's headed paper for him to provide to prospective employers. Alternatively, the agreement may be that the employer will retain the agreed reference and provide it in direct response to requests from prospective employers. The agreement could extend to include an undertaking by the company that any oral references will be in terms no less favourable than the agreed form reference. The agreed reference should be attached to the compromise agreement (see para 4.1 of Appendix C, p 123).

Confidentiality and post-termination restrictions

The compromise agreement should include express reference to any obligations in relation to confidentiality and restrictions on certain post-termination activities. The starting point is to refer to the executive's employment contract, which will hopefully include restrictive covenants and express terms covering the ongoing requirement to safeguard the confidentiality of certain information (such as trade secrets and other information which can be properly desribed as confidential). Even where the employment contract contains satisfactory terms on confidentiality and restrictions, it is sensible to reaffirm the terms in the compromise agreement. Where the employment contract does not contain such terms, or if they are considered to be unenforceable, the company may want to introduce new terms designed to protect its legitimate business interests.

Chapter 7 sets out the categories of confidential information which can be protected post-termination of employment and also examines post-termination restrictions. If the company has already taken the opportunity to protect its business by putting the executive on garden leave for all or part of his notice period (see Chaps 3 and 7) bear this in mind when considering whether to introduce new covenants.

If the company proposes to introduce new covenants, is there any consideration being provided to the executive in exchange for his acceptance of them (see above)? If money is to be paid for a *new* covenant, it will be taxable (see Chap 6). This is not the case where the compromise agreement simply reaffirms existing covenants. To avoid prejudicing the tax treatment of the whole termination payment, it is preferable to attribute an amount as consideration for acceptance of the new restriction, accepting that such consideration will be fully taxable.

Assistance

The company may need the executive's assistance in the future in relation to possible legal proceedings. If so, the company should include a provision in the compromise agreement requiring the executive to give such assistance. It is a matter for negotiation whether the company agrees to pay the executive an allowance per day or meet his reasonable out of pocket expenses incurred in giving such assistance.

Settlement

The company should ensure that it obtains from the executive an overall settlement of all claims the latter may have against the company, companies in the same group (where appropriate) and other officers and employees of the company (bearing in mind the points made above in relation to what claims a compromise agreement can be used to settle).

Senior executives may try to negotiate making the full and final settlement term mutual. The company may not be willing to agree, especially if it does not appreciate what claims may be involved. If the company is prepared to agree to a mutual full and final settlement provision, it should be limited to those claims which the company knows about as at a particular date.

5.4 **Role of ACAS and arbitration**

Once tribunal proceedings have been issued an ACAS officer is usually assigned to the case. The ACAS conciliation officer can assist with without prejudice negotiations and can formally document the terms of settlement in a form COT3. ACAS conciliation officers will not usually become involved in without prejudice negotiations in the context of an executive severance. This is because commonly the negotiations can be conducted and a settlement concluded without the need for the executive to issue tribunal proceedings. Also, historically, the £12,000 cap on the amount of compensation which could be awarded for a successful claim of unfair dismissal meant that asserting this statutory claim was not of greatest importance to the executive. The increase in the cap on unfair dismissal compensation is likely to encourage executives to assert potential unfair dismissal claims. In this context, new proposals for an arbitration scheme may be of interest to both executives and their former employers.

These proposals were set out in ERDRA. They relate to setting up a scheme designed to promote arbitration in unfair dismissal disputes (wrongful dismissal and discrimination disputes are not included). The aim is to provide a voluntary alternative to the employment tribunal with the attractions of the arbitration route being that the employer and executive will have a more informal, speedy, private and less expensive means of settling their dispute. This may be of interest to both parties particularly where the company wishes to settle the matter with the minimum fuss and risk of adverse publicity.

Given that the aims underlying the proposed arbitration scheme were those attributed to the employment tribunal system when it was first established, it remains to be seen whether the arbitration system will live up to the stated aim of providing an informal and speedy dispute resolution route.

Key points

In documenting the severance terms consider:

- what claims (statutory, contractual or otherwise) are in issue;
- the form the severance agreement will take;
- whether the company requires the executive to sign a compromise agreement;
- what will be the termination date;
- what must be paid up to the termination date;
- the manner of payment and tax treatment of the termination payment;

- whether any benefits will be continued;
- whether the executive needs to resign a directorship(s);
- including post-termination obligations including return of company property; safeguarding confidentiality, restrictive covenants;
- will there be an agreed reference or agreed announcements;
- whether all conditions relating to compromise agreements have been satisfied;
- will the company contribute towards the executive's legal fees?

Chapter 6

· **Costing the Deal** ·

6.1 **Introduction**

The issues which arise on termination of an executive's employment are many and complex. In addition to considering the usual issues which arise on the termination of employment of less senior employees, (for example, the reason for the dismissal, any legal claims which may arise and the likely award which the employee may receive if successful in either the courts or the employment tribunal), the company may be concerned with issues of adverse publicity, and in the case of public companies whether the severance will have repercussions affecting the share price and issues of compliance with the London Stock Exchange Rules and other regulatory bodies. This chapter focuses on the basic principles relating to calculating damages and the value of the severance package.

6.2 **What are the legal claims?**

A severance package will arise from a termination of an executive's employment and its value is usually referable to a greater or lesser degree to the executive's legal rights. As has already been mentioned, on termination, the executive usually has two sets of rights, namely:

(1) Rights arising under the employment contract (of which the principal claim is usually for damages for wrongful dismissal);
(2) Statutory rights (principally unfair dismissal, sex, race or disability discrimination and claims under Part II of the Employment Rights Act 1996 for payment of wages).

Contractual rights

Any employee who is dismissed without notice or prior to the expiry of a fixed term may be able to claim damages for breach of contract. This is a claim for wrongful dismissal and it will succeed unless there were grounds for dismissal without notice (*e.g.* by reason of gross misconduct).

Where a company considers there are grounds to dismiss without notice, it would be usual to terminate the executive's employment without notice or pay in lieu of notice. Even where there are grounds for instant dismissal, this will not necessarily prevent the executive from bringing a claim challenging the basis of dismissal. Accordingly, if the company wants to defend a potential wrongful dismissal claim, it is important to ensure that the executive's employment contract entitles the company to dismiss without notice in the circumstances which have arisen.

An executive who is wrongfully dismissed is entitled to recover sufficient damages to place him in the same position as if the employment had been terminated lawfully. Usually, this will be limited to the remuneration (salary and benefits) which the executive has been prevented from earning or enjoying for the part of any notice period which has not been worked or for the balance of the fixed term. In *Shove* v *Downs Surgical plc* [1984] ICR 532 the court approved a method of calculating these losses which is now widely followed:

- the calculation consists of an assessment of the gross value of salary and benefits which would have been paid/received for the notice period/balance of fixed term;
- once this first stage of the calculation is complete, the tax and national insurance which would have been deducted had notice/balance of fixed term been worked are deducted, which then leaves a net loss figure. This figure will then be adjusted to take account of any earnings the executive received or is likely to receive during the unworked portion of the notice period/fixed term, to mitigate or reduce the potential loss. There will also be a further reduction for accelerated receipt (or early payment) and contingencies;
- this leaves a final net loss figure. After assessing whether any part of the severance is exempt from tax, the balance of the payment should be grossed up for tax so that after deducting all tax payable the executive is left with a sum equivalent to his net loss figure.

In *Shove* v *Downs Surgical plc* Mr Shove brought a claim for wrongful dismissal following his summary dismissal as sole managing director of the company. Mr Shove was entitled to 30 months' notice under his contract of employment. In awarding damages the court estimated the net amount which would have been received by Mr Shove after deduction of income tax from his gross income and then added an amount equivalent to his estimated income tax, so that the net amount represented, as realistically as possible, the actual loss suffered. The court concluded that Mr Shove was entitled to damages of £60,729 (after deductions for mitigation and to reflect the fact that he was receiving a lump sum payment). In order to ensure that Mr Shove was left with that amount the court awarded damages of £83,477 to take account of the tax payable on the compensation.

The more recent decision in *Clark* v *BET* [1997] IRLR 348 will have a significant impact on the first stage of the calculation of the losses suffered by an executive who is wrongfully dismissed, namely the gross value of the salary and benefits which he would have received for the notice period or balance of the fixed term. Many of the issues which arose for consideration in that case involved determining to what Mr Clark was entitled under the terms of his employment contract. For example, as Mr Clark was employed under a three-year rolling contract, the court awarded him three years' salary with an annual increase in salary of 10%. This was notwithstanding the fact that the employment contract provided that salary would only be increased by such amount, if any, as the board in its absolute discretion would decide.

The impact of the *Clark* case will be considered further below.

Other possible contractual claims include:

- accrued but unpaid salary and holiday pay;
- entitlement to bonus or commission;
- unpaid expenses;
- dismissal in breach of a contractual procedure (for example disciplinary including appeals or grievance);
- PHI benefits on a termination for ill health.

Where there has been a termination in breach of contract, the executive may raise as part of a claim for damages for wrongful dismissal, the issue of damage to reputation. It was not possible until relatively recently to raise such a head of claim. However, the House of Lords ruled in *Malik and Another* v *BCCI* [1997] IRLR 462 that where an employer's conduct breaches the implied contractual term of mutual trust and confidence and that breach causes financial loss to the executive as a result of damage to his reputation, compensation is recoverable (see also Chap 2). In the *Malik* case the potential breach of contract was that BCCI had conducted its business in a dishonest way. The employees in that case argued that they were tainted with their former employer's dishonesty and that therefore it was difficult to find future employment.

Claims for unpaid sums due under the employment contract can be brought in the county court, High Court or in the employment tribunal (under Part II of the Employment Rights Act 1996 (formerly the Wages Act 1986)) or under the tribunal's jurisdiction to hear breach of contract claims up to a value of £25,000. Although the principal remedy for wrongful dismissal is damages, the courts do have power to grant equitable or discretionary remedies, *e.g.* an injunction to prevent a dismissal in breach of a contractual procedure or a declaration that a dismissal is or would be wrongful in breach of contract. In practice, however, claims for equitable relief are relatively rare.

Statutory rights

The executive may also qualify for statutory employment protection rights, such as the right not to be unfairly dismissed or the right not to suffer discrimination on the grounds of the executive's sex, race or disability.

Unfair dismissal

To be eligible to claim unfair dismissal, the executive must meet certain requirements, the most well known of which is to have the necessary continuous employment with the company or an associated company. Other requirements are that the executive must:

- not ordinarily work outside Great Britain;
- not have waived his rights under a fixed-term contract (fixed-term contracts of at least one year or more may include a waiver provision which, provided the contract is signed by the executive, will prevent the executive from claiming unfair dismissal if the contract ends simply by the expiry of the fixed term*);
- not have reached the normal retirement age for his employer (or 65 if there is no normal retirement age);
- not have settled a potential or actual unfair dismissal claim in accordance with section 203 of the Employment Rights Act 1996 (see Chap 5).

Note that at the time of writing the Government proposed, as part of its Employment Relations Bill, to abolish the waiver of unfair dismissal rights in fixed term contracts.

Although the primary remedy for unfair dismissal is an order for re-engagement or reinstatement, the most common remedy is financial compensation. At the time of writing the changes to the limits on compensation for unfair dismissal proposed by the Government under Fairness at Work had not taken effect. Therefore references to current maximums are to the limits before the changes take effect, although as far as possible reference to the proposed changes has been included.

Unfair dismissal compensation consists of two parts:

Basic award

This is a statutory calculation which is determined without reference to any actual losses the executive has sustained. It is a simple calculation based on the executive's number of years' service and age and is identical to the calculation of statutory redundancy pay. The formula is:

- one and a half week's pay for each year of employment in which the executive was aged 41 or over;
- one week's pay for each year of employment in which the executive was aged 22-40;
- half a week's pay for each year of employment in which the executive was aged below 22 (for redundancy count only years when the individual was aged 18 or over).

The maximum weekly pay which can be taken into account is currently £220 (under the Government's Fairness at Work proposals, this will be index-linked). The maximum number of years' service which may be taken into account is 20 (counting later years before earlier years). This gives a current maximum basic award of £6,600 (see below – compensation changes under Fairness at Work). The employment tribunal may reduce the basic award where:

- the executive has unreasonably refused an offer of reinstatement;
- it is just and equitable to do so in the light of the executive's conduct before dismissal;
- the dismissal was due to redundancy and the executive has received a redundancy payment.

Compensatory award

This award compensates the executive for losses sustained in consequence of the dismissal, insofar as that loss is attributable to action taken by the employer. This is usually the executive's actual losses arising after the termination date, for which he has not already been compensated or which have not been set off by any earnings which he has had since the termination. The current maximum compensatory award is £12,000 (proposed to rise to £50,000).

The compensatory award covers various heads of loss as follows:

- the executive's loss of earnings from the date of dismissal to the date of hearing;
- future loss of earnings beyond the date of the tribunal hearing;
- loss of pension rights (in calculating this the employment tribunal may refer to a guidance booklet called "Industrial Tribunals – Compensation for Loss of Pension Rights". This guidance does not have statutory force);
- loss of statutory employment rights acquired through length of continuous service (this usually amounts to a fixed figure of around £150 for loss of statutory protection and an amount equal to half the net pay for half of the statutory notice period to compensate for loss of accrued statutory notice rights).

The compensatory award is not intended to punish the employer. It reflects the actual loss suffered by the executive and accordingly will be reduced by any sums which reduce the executive's loss, for example:

- payments received on termination;
- income received from new employment after dismissal;
- unemployment benefit.

The compensatory award may be reduced in other ways:

- where there is contributory fault by the executive;
- where dismissal probably would have happened even if a proper procedure had been followed (known as a *Polkey* reduction – see also Chap 2).

Note the order of deductions is summarised below.

Compensatory awards may also be affected after 1 January 1999 by section 13 of the Employment Rights (Dispute Resolution) Act 1998. This allows the employment tribunal to reduce the compensatory award if an executive does not make use of an internal appeal procedure. However, the compensatory award may be enhanced if the employer prevents an executive using such an appeal procedure.

Prior to the Government's Fairness at Work proposals taking effect, compensation in an unfair dismissal case could be increased by either a special or an additional award. The Government proposed simplifying this system by consolidating additional and special awards so that it will only be possible in future for tribunals to make an additional award. In the past such awards were rarely made by tribunals as they relate to circumstances where the company refused to comply with an order made by the tribunal to re-employ the individual. Given the relative rarity of these awards what follows is a short summary of additional awards as they will operate after the Government implements its proposed change.

Additional award

Where an employer refuses to comply with a re-employment order made by the employment tribunal, an additional award may be made. The amount will be between 26 and 52 weeks' pay (a week's pay being limited to a maximum of £220 which will be index-linked).

Order of deductions

There have been a number of cases on the order of deductions. Cases have taken different approaches which have resulted in very different outcomes in terms of the final award. Where the executive has received an *ex-gratia* payment or a redundancy payment or if there is any reduction to be made either because of contributory fault or to reflect the fact that following a fair procedure would have made no difference to the decision to dismiss (the *Polkey* reduction), it is important to consider in which order these deductions should be made. On the basis of the most recent cases (the EAT decision in *Heggie* v *Uniroyal Englebert Tyres Ltd* [1998] IRLR 425 and *Digital Equipment Co Ltd* v *Clements (No 2)* [1998] ICR 258) the approach to making deductions is as follows:

- **redundancy payment:** first calculate the actual loss, then make any *Polkey* reduction and finally deduct any enhanced redundancy payment;
- **other dismissals:** first calculate the actual loss, then reduce for any contributory fault and finally deduct any *ex-gratia* payment.

In both cases, the statutory cap should only be applied after the deductions have been made.

Compensation changes under Fairness at Work

Historically when negotiating severance packages with directors and senior executives the potential compensation for unfair dismissal was more often than not ignored. Severance packages have tended to be based on the executive's contractual rights as these have usually been worth more to the executive in terms of a potential claim than statutory rights (given the cap of £12,000 on unfair dismissal compensation and assuming there was no element of discrimination involved).

However, this is likely to change in the future. The Fairness at Work White Paper (published in May 1998) proposed abolishing the upper limit on unfair dismissal compensation. Since then the Government has declared that rather than abolishing the limit altogether, it should be raised to £50,000 and thereafter index-linked. In addition it has been proposed that the amount of a week's pay (current maximum of £220) for tribunal awards should be index-linked. This will affect the amount of basic and additional awards. If this proposal is implemented, executives will still be able to pursue their contractual rights. However, the prospect of an enhanced maximum limit for compensation for unfair dismissal is likely to entice executives to make unfair dismissal claims where they had previously not done so. Executives' claims will essentially be for future loss, *i.e.* the loss they will suffer over and above that covered by their contractual rights. Significant claims for future loss would arise in the following situations:

- executives whose employment commenced before the pensions cap (see below for further discussion) was introduced in 1989. If their employment is now terminated they will lose the very valuable benefit of uncapped pension arrangements. To match these in any new employment the new employer would have to provide an unapproved retirement benefit scheme. Some do this, but not all. For the executive whose uncapped pension arrangements are not matched, his future loss of pension benefit will be potentially very substantial indeed. There will be nothing to prevent a claim for the loss of these benefits being made in an unfair dismissal claim;
- executives who are unlikely to obtain employment on a similar package to that enjoyed previously will be able to claim loss of the differential in earnings. This could be based on discretionary as well as contractual earnings. For example, if they enjoyed substantial discretionary bonuses in their

previous employment, they may be able to include the loss of these in an unfair dismissal claim;

- those who face the prospect of not being able to obtain employment again. This is most likely to be individuals whose employment is terminated within, say, 10 years of retirement. They may be able to obtain some non-executive directorships but their loss of earnings will of course be substantial if they do not find equivalent full time employment.

In the past, companies have been able to minimise the risk of litigation from departing executives by including in the employment contract pay in lieu of notice provisions or liquidated damages clauses. These pre-determine the sum of money that will be paid to the executive on termination and often state that they will be paid in full and final settlement of all claims. Under the Employment Rights Act 1996 such provisions cannot be worded so as to contract out of statutory employment protection rights thus preventing unfair dismissal claims being made. However, there may be some pratical incentive for the executive not to bring statutory claims in such circumstances. An increase in the cap will also prompt more complex calculations of loss for unfair dismissal purposes particularly as far as pension loss is concerned.

Relationship between wrongful and unfair dismissal damages

If an executive brings claims for both wrongful dismissal and unfair dismissal, he will not be allowed to recover for the same loss twice and this will be taken into account by either the court or the employment tribunal when assessing compensation. However, that will not prevent recovery of damages for unfair dismissal as well as wrongful dismissal (*O'Laoire* v *Jackel International Ltd* [1990] IRLR 70). Whilst damages for wrongful dismissal are limited to the notice period or balance of the fixed term, unfair dismissal damages are not limited to a particular period and can be awarded for periods beyond the end of the notice period or fixed term, provided the executive can show continued loss. Another reason which may enable executives, particularly high earners to recover both wrongful dismissal damages and the maximum compensatory award arises because the methods which the employment tribunal uses to calculate certain losses, particularly pension loss, differ from the approach commonly followed by the courts. The issue of recovering unfair dismissal damages in addition to those for wrongful dismissal will become an increasingly important aspect of negotiating the severance package after the Employment Relations Bill is implemented.

Discrimination

If there is any element of either sexual or racial discrimination or discrimination on the grounds of disability in the termination, the executive may be entitled to recover unlimited compensation for financial loss and a further award for injury to feelings.

In discrimination cases the employment tribunal may also:

- award aggravated damages if the discriminator has acted in a high-handed, malicious, insulting or oppressive manner;
- make a declaration of the parties' rights;
- make a recommendation (the aim of this is to minimise the adverse impact of the discrimination on the complainant).

If a dismissal is both unfair and discriminatory the effect as far as compensation is concerned is that the statutory cap on the compensatory award element of unfair dismissal is lifted.

Injury to feelings

Awards for injury to feelings vary a great deal and can be very high for particularly blatant or nasty acts of discrimination (including harassment). The Employment Appeal Tribunal (EAT) has given guidance on the approach to be adopted when assessing injury to feelings awards:

- the awards should be compensatory, not punitive;
- they should not be too low, to avoid lessening respect for discrimination legislation;
- they should be broadly similar to the range of awards in personal injury cases;
- tribunals should remind themselves of the everyday value of such awards;
- the level of awards should command public respect.

This guidance was given in *Armitage, Marsden & HM Prison Service* v *Johnson* [1997] IRLR 162 where the award was £20,000 for injury to feelings. Since then higher injury to feelings awards have been made;

most recently an award of £40,000 paid to Mr Yeboah the former head of personnel services at Hackney Council. His overall compensation was £380,000.

A limit of £12,000 on the compensatory award for unfair dismissal provided an incentive for an executive to assert discrimination claims as compensation for discrimination is not capped in any way. This practice will not necessarily end with a higher cap for unfair dismissal of £50,000 in place.

Deductions from wages

An executive who is dismissed may try to bring a claim in the employment tribunal in respect of sums to which he believes he is contractually entitled under Part II of the Employment Rights Act 1996. Note that there is no upper limit on the amount which may be recovered this way provided the sum claimed arises due to an unlawful deduction from wages. A recent example of an executive making use of this statutory claim in the employment tribunal was Mary Walz, the former Barings director and global head of equity financial products (which included the derivatives operation in which Nick Leeson traded in Singapore). She claimed an unpaid bonus of £500,000 and argued that the bonus, the amount of which she was told the day before the news about Nick Leeson's activities broke in the press, was a contractual entitlement, the non-payment of which amounted to an unlawful deduction.

Having considered the potential legal claims, we now look at calculating the value of the severance sum.

6.3 **Assessing value of severance package**

On an executive termination the amount of money paid to the executive in the form of a severance package will usually be a matter for negotiation. Accordingly, whilst the company should try to assess the amount the executive would be entitled to, assuming his potential claims (whether under his contract or under statute) were successful, bear in mind that the final figure will frequently be the result of a horse trade and nor merely a reflection of actual loss. The horsetrade will not always focus on or even involve the severance amount itself. Negotiation may revolve around other features of the settlement deal (for example, whether the company will meet all or part of the executive's legal or other professional fees; whether the company will provide outplacement consultancy for the executive, inclusion of restrictive covenants, whether there will be an agreed reference etc).

In negotiating the severance figure, companies must bear in mind any limitations on their freedom to increase the amount. For example, where the executive is a director for the purposes of the Companies Acts, *prior* shareholder approval must be sought for payments made as compensation for loss of office (s 312, Companies Act 1985) except where the payment is:

- bona fide damages; or
- paid by way of pension in respect of past services.

(s 316(3), Companies Act 1985). Note also the *Taupo Totoro Timber Co Ltd* v *Rowe* [1978] AC 537 exception (payments which the company is contractually bound to make will not be unlawful by virtue of s312).

As part of its preparation before effecting an executive termination, the company should assess the value of the severance package so that it can decide what offer to make to the executive.

6.4 General principles

The common starting point for any severance package is to assess the value of the executive's claim for wrongful dismissal and, to a lesser degree, unfair dismissal.

In assessing the values of these claims the employer should consider:

- the remuneration lost (remuneration being net salary and the after tax value of benefits to which the executive was contractually entitled); and
- the period of loss. This will be the executive's notice period or the balance of the fixed term in the case of wrongful dismissal or some longer period in the case of unfair dismissal.

Wrongful dismissal

The period of loss (*i.e.* the notice period or the balance of the fixed term) is usually ascertained by looking at the contract of employment. If there is no written contract and the contract is neither for a fixed term nor has a notice period been agreed, the contract may be terminated on *reasonable* notice. What will be reasonable in any given case will depend on a number of factors:

- length of service;
- seniority;
- remuneration;
- age;
- what is usual for the particular industry/profession;
- size of the employer;

Notice should not be less than the minimum statutory periods. Minimum statutory notice is as follows:

continuous employment for one month or more but less than two years;	one week's notice.
continuous employment for two years or more;	one week's notice for each year of continuous employment up to a maximum of 12 weeks for 12 years or more.

In rough terms reasonable notice for managers and even directors of small private companies would be from three to six months whereas for executives of larger private companies and public companies it would be between six months and a year. Note that the Hampel Committee's Code of Best Practice recommends notice periods of not more than one year for executive directors of public companies.

Where the executive has been dismissed in breach of the employer's contractual disciplinary rules he may also claim damages in relation to the period that it would have taken for the procedure to be followed and employment to be terminated lawfully.

Unfair dismissal

The period of loss in unfair dismissal cases will depend on factors such as:

- whether or not the executive is likely to obtain future employment;
- if so, the length of time it will be before he obtains such employment; and
- the age and seniority of the executive.

What is the loss?

Before looking at some individual aspects of remuneration it is important to bear in mind some general principles.

In deciding what salary and benefits the executive would have enjoyed during the notice period/balance of fixed term, is the company obliged to take account of potential future increases or improvements in salary and/or benefits? For many years it was thought not. The principle that a party should not be liable for "not doing that which he is not bound to do" established in *Lavarack* v *Woods of Colchester* [1967] QB 278, CA resulted in the assumption that damages should be assessed according to the company's contractual liability at the date employment terminates, and not on the basis of what the executive *might* have received during the notice period/balance of fixed term. This approach was challenged in *BET* v *Clark* [1997] IRLR 348 in relation to the assessment of loss of salary, bonus etc. This challenge is perhaps best illustrated by the example of the assessment of loss of basic salary.

Example

Mr Clark had a three-year rolling contract which provided that salary "shall be reviewed annually and be increased by such amount if any as the Board shall in its absolute discretion decide". There was, therefore, a contractual right not only to an annual review but also to a salary increase following each review. The company's discretion was limited to determining the amount of that increase. Given this, the High Court rejected the company's argument that Mr Clark would not have received a salary increase over the notice period. To have exercised discretion so that Mr Clark received a nil increase would have been in bad faith and a breach of contract. After considering the evidence that Mr Clark had in the past received increases of approximately 10% per annum and on other issues, such as the fact that executives still at the company would have increases in salary in the future in line with future profit forecasts, the court held that Mr Clark would have received an annual salary increase of 10% for each year of his notice.

Note that the principles in *Lavarack* have not been entirely displaced by the *Clark* case. There will not be a right to damages in respect of future salary increases where there is no contractual right to an increase. However, where there is such a right the employer's contractual obligations will not now necessarily be construed in the manner least burdensome for the employer. This could have a significant impact, not only in terms of salary, but also as far as bonus is concerned (see below).

The employer should also have regard to the legal principle that where a party suffers a loss by reason of a breach of contract, the party should be placed in the same situation with respect to damages as if the contract had been performed. Accordingly, the value of employment benefits should be calculated from the executive's point of view by considering the market cost to him of purchasing equivalent benefits (*i.e.* what would it cost the executive, for example, if he were to obtain medical insurance or life cover following termination of employment, which provided benefits equal to those provided under his employment contract?). The cost to the employer of providing the benefit during employment will usually be less because of discounts available for group policies (but is often used in the calculation by the employer since the figures will be readily available).

It is common to allow certain benefits to continue after termination of employment as part of the terms of a severance agreement. However, the employer must consider the costs implications of continuing to provide benefits as well as whether or not it is appropriate, or indeed possible, to continue benefits once employment has terminated. On a practical level, it may be that certain benefits cannot be continued once employment has terminated. For example, where the executive is a member of an occupational pension scheme it would not normally be possible to continue active membership once employment has ended. The same difficulty arises with life assurance where provision of the benefit is linked to membership of an occupational pension scheme.

Methods have been developed to calculate the loss of certain benefits. Note that loss relates only to the *private* value of a benefit. For example, if a company car is provided solely for use to perform work, there will be no private benefit to the executive and therefore no loss in this respect on termination of employment.

Note that the generally accepted means of calculating loss of salary and benefits to take account of taxation (as approved in *Shove* v *Downs Surgical plc* [1984] ICR 352) is set out above.

In assessing the value of the remuneration lost for the notice period/balance of the fixed term take account of the following elements of remuneration:

- basic salary (including pay rises);
- commission;

- bonus;
- company car;
- holiday pay;
- pension.

Are any of the following claims/heads of loss (which do not necessarily arise from the executive's employment contract) recoverable?

- injury to reputation;
- injury to feelings;
- compensation for loss of job security;
- breach of a contractual disciplinary/termination procedure.

There may be other ways in which the value of the severance package may be increased, such as:

- outplacement;
- legal or other professional fees;
- payment for acceptance of restrictive covenants.

Finally, the severance package may be reduced to take account of mitigation or accelerated receipt and tax must be deducted where necessary. Remember that the executive may have statutory claims (*e.g.* unfair dismissal discrimination and unlawful deductions from wages) in respect of which the amount of compensation is not limited by the notice period or balance of the fixed term of the contract as the case may be.

6.5 **Assessing lost remuneration**

Basic salary (including pay rises)

As explained above damages for wrongful dismissal are assessed according to the terms of the employment contract. The starting point in calculating damages for loss of basic salary is to work out how much the executive would have earned (after deductions) during the notice period/balance of fixed term. Whether the company should base this calculation on the amount of the executive's salary as at the date of employment without taking account of pay increases which may have been awarded during the notice period/balance of fixed term will depend on terms of the executive's employment contract interpreted in line with the *Clark* decision that the company can no longer rely on performing only its minimum contractual obligations. Whilst it remains the case that there must be a contractual obligation (a reasonable expectation of an increase is not sufficient), executives should rely on the *Clark* case to argue that the loss of base salary should be increased by future upwards pay reviews.

Commission

In assessing compensation for wrongful dismissal the damages to which an executive is entitled will not necessarily be calculated on the basis that the company's business would have continued to flourish. In *Roberts* v *Elwell Engineers Ltd* [1972] 2 QB 586 the court found that commission was payable beyond the end of the three-month notice period but that allowance had to be made for the vicissitudes of trade and the likelihood of the company's receiving repeat orders from customers introduced by the employee. A reasonable yardstick for assessing lost commission would be the employee's average commission earnings before the dismissal. The question of commission did not arise in the *Clark* case.

Bonus

Bonus could form a potentially large element of the damages. A lot will depend on the nature of the bonus scheme, or how the bonus entitlement has been expressed – in both cases whether bonus is contractual, discretionary or a mixture of the two. Where bonuses are wholly discretionary they should be ignored by the employer when negotiating the severance package. However, it will be a head of loss where there is no discretion or the element of discretion is limited and executives have contractual rights; for example:

- where the employer has discretion as to who to invite to participate in the bonus scheme, but having been invited, the executive has the right to participate; or
- the employer has the discretion to withdraw/discontinue the bonus scheme but until it is discontinued, the executive has the right to participate.

Where compensation for bonus is to be included, the calculation will depend on a number of factors including the rules of the scheme (if any), whether there is a given formula for bonuses and whether it is possible to forecast what the bonus would have been had the executive continued to be employed for the notice period/fixed term.

Recent cases

The following cases illustrate situations where damages for loss of bonus were awarded.

In the *Clark* case, John Clark had a contractual right to participate in a bonus scheme which provided for a maximum bonus of 60% of salary. Mr Clark claimed damages on the basis that he would have received a bonus of 60% of salary for each year of his notice period. The company argued he would have received no bonus at all or a bonus of only 6%. The court accepted there was a contractual right for Mr Clark to receive bonus and rejected the company's argument that the company was entitled to perform the contract in the manner most favourable to the company (*i.e.* by awarding little or no bonus). The court had to decide what position Mr Clark would have been in if the company had performed the contract properly. In order to make a realistic assessment of what Mr Clark would have received, the court looked at the bonuses which Mr Clark had previously earned, those earned by the chief executive and finance director of the company and the likely future bonuses which would be paid to the company's executives. Mr Clark was awarded a bonus of 50% of salary for his three-year notice period.

In *Noble Enterprises Ltd* v *Lieberum*, EAT, 23 June 1998 a bonus scheme was found to be contractual rather than discretionary despite the fact that the employer was not obliged to operate the scheme every year. One of the difficulties here was that the scheme was not written down. Looking at the employer's practice it was clear that the scheme had operated for a number of years without a break. Further, the employer had to say in advance if it did not want to operate the scheme in a particular year. Both these issues meant the employer failed in arguing that no bonus was payable in circumstances where employment ended before the bonus payment date.

A recent case has made clear that where there is a discretion to award bonus, failure to award a bonus in a termination situation will not necessarily amount to a breach of contract. In *Midland Bank plc* v *McCann*, EAT, 23 July 1998 the employer's refusal to pay a discretionary bonus to an individual who was under notice of redundancy, was not in breach of contract. The particular bonus scheme terms indicated that it was designed to motivate employees.

Given this, the employer had not acted in bad faith or exercised its discretion capriciously in refusing any bonus payment.

Company car

It is important to establish from the contract whether the executive has a contractual right to use the company car for private as well as business purposes. Where the executive is only entitled to the car for business purposes, there will be no claim for damages in relation to loss of the car on termination. The loss of car was considered in *Shove* v *Downs Surgical plc*. The executive's contract provided for him to have a Daimler car and the court found that he was contractually entitled to the car for private use and to recover the cost of his private petrol. The court relied on evidence from the annual AA tables as to the cost of running cars of various sizes having rejected other means of assessing the executive's loss. The court rejected assessing loss by reference to:

- the tax on company cars as determined by tax legislation on the basis that such a method of assessment did not actually reflect the executive's loss;
- what sort of car the executive might reasonably be expected to acquire in his present circumstances as Mr Shove's contract expressly provided for him to have a Daimler; and
- the cost of buying a year old Daimler and running costs for the whole of Mr Shove's notice period.

In Mr Shove's case, compensation was assessed on the basis his private mileage was no more than 5,000 miles per year. He received £10,000 in damages. Mr Clark was also entitled to a car for both business and private use. On the facts, however, it was established that Mr Clark made very little private use of his car. His award of £2,000 damages per annum reflected this minimal use. Now it is common to assess loss by reference to the Inland Revenue scale rates for car and fuel rather than the AA tables (which generally produce a figure less than the taxable benefit).

Holiday pay

Historically, claims for holiday pay arose from the terms of the contract. However, since the Working Time Regulations 1998 took effect in the United Kingdom on 1 October 1998, all workers, including executives, have been entitled to minimum paid annual leave (20 days from November 1999) and to be paid in lieu of any such accrued, untaken holiday when employment ends, irrespective of the reason for termination. The employment contract cannot be used to avoid working time rules on minimum holiday and payment in lieu of it on termination. Thus, contract terms providing that there is no entitlement to accrued holiday pay if the reason for termination is gross misconduct or where the executive resigns without giving proper notice are probably no longer enforceable. However, the terms of the contract will still be relevant in relation to holiday over and above minimum working time holiday.

Employment contracts often provide that in a termination accrued holiday is to be taken during the notice period. Therefore, there will be no entitlement to pay in lieu of accrued holiday on termination. In *Whittle Contractors Ltd v Smith*, EAT, 842/94, Mr Smith took voluntary redundancy and was on garden leave for two months. He was not paid accrued holiday pay on termination as his employer argued that in accordance with an express term of the contract, Mr Smith must be regarded as having taken accrued holiday whilst on garden leave. The EAT disagreed. It concluded that just because Mr Smith had been on garden leave and paid for that, he had not lost the right to be paid in lieu of holiday pay which had accrued up to the date of termination.

Pension

Pension loss may be an important (and large) element of the damages. The starting point is to establish the executive's contractual entitlement by looking at the employment contract. It is also important to consider the rules of the particular pension scheme. The loss itself should be assessed in terms of the value of the executive's continued membership of the scheme during the period of loss.

In cases of wrongful dismissal the period of loss will be the contractual notice period or balance of the fixed term. In unfair dismissal cases the executive may have a future loss over and above the loss arising in respect of the contractual notice period/fixed term.

The appropriate approach to assessing loss will depend on the type of pension scheme:

Final salary/defined benefit scheme

The executive's loss is the cost of the difference between the capitalised value of the executive's pension at the date of termination and what it would have been at the point of expiry of the contractual notice period or fixed term;

Money purchase/defined contribution

The executive's loss is usually estimated as the prospective value of the employer's further contributions over the period of loss. The same principle applies to both occupational schemes and personal pension schemes.

Assessment of pension loss can be potentially complex because of the actuarial problems in deciding on the amount to award the executive to compensate for the loss of future entitlement.

Where the executive is not a member of an occupational pension scheme, but the employer has paid contributions during the period of employment to the individual's approved personal pension scheme, the employer cannot pay contributions direct to a personal pension scheme after the executive's employment has ended. Where settlement negotiations commence after the executive has already been dismissed, any sums to be paid in respect of loss of pension payment will have to be paid direct to the executive who will then be able to pay the money into his personal pension scheme using his tax relief allowances. In the case of payments into a personal pension scheme, the executive should have in mind his Inland Revenue limit (which varies according to the age of the individual). The limits are currently as follows:

Age	Percentage of net relevant earnings which may be contributed per tax year
16 – 35	17.5
36 – 45	20
46 – 50	25
51 – 55	30
56 – 60	35
61 and over	40

In addition to the arrangements made by the employer to compensate the executive for pension loss the executive may request that part of any lump sum compensation be paid into pension. This is possible in the case of both occupational and personal pension schemes where the executive is below Inland Revenue limits and is particularly relevant where the total damages payable on termination to the individual exceeds £30,000. If the excess over £30,000 can be paid into the pension scheme without exceeding Inland Revenue limits it is possible to avoid or reduce any charge to tax on the severance package.

The earnings cap (introduced by the Finance Act 1989) means that executives who joined an approved pension scheme after 1989 can only receive pensions through approved schemes based on salary up to the cap which is currently £90,600. Executives who have uncapped pensions as a result of having been a member of an approved pension scheme prior to 1989 will become subject to the Inland Revenue cap if they move jobs on termination of employment. Becoming capped can involve significant loss in terms of future pension contributions for executives earning in excess of the cap. Where such an executive seeks a large sum in compensation for loss of an uncapped pension, the employer may argue that the application of the cap is as a result of overriding legislation and not a breach of contract. In addition, the employer might be able to argue that the executive is likely to be able to mitigate his or her loss by any new employer setting up an unapproved pension scheme in addition to any approved occupational scheme of which the executive may become a member.

The employment tribunals published guidelines on their approach to calculating compensation for loss of pension rights in 1991. The guidelines state that the method used should be comprehensible and acceptable to ordinary litigants and should assess three categories of loss:

- loss of pension rights from the date of dismissal to the hearing;
- loss of future pension rights from the hearing to the date of retirement; and
- loss of enhancement of accrued pension rights (in general this will relate to final salary schemes rather than company money purchase schemes or personal pension plans).

The guidelines suggest that, in unfair dismissal cases, it may be preferable to assess the basic and compensatory awards without reference to loss of pension rights. This is because the £12,000 limit on compensation has meant that a highly paid executive may well reach it without considering his lost pension rights. This is not, however, going to be the case with a compensatory cap of £50,000.

Share option rights

If the executive participates in a share option scheme, on termination, the executive may try to seek compensation for loss of share options. As with other benefits it is important to establish what, if any, rights the executive has under the scheme. Are there contractual rights and are rights expressed to lapse on termination of employment (irrespective of the reason for termination) or do they survive termination? Where the executive has a contractual right in relation to the share option scheme, loss arising from the right may form part of damages. However, many schemes contain an exclusion providing that the executive will not be entitled to be compensated for lost rights under the scheme. Such an exclusion was tested in the case of *Micklefield v SAC Technology Ltd* [1990] 1 All ER 275 .

Mr Micklefield was granted an option under the company's share option scheme. Under the terms of the scheme not only was the option to lapse if he ceased to be employed for any reason but also there was an exclusion of liability for compensation for loss of any rights under the option scheme arising on termination of employment for any reason. When he was dismissed, Mr Micklefield claimed damages for wrongful dismissal including loss of rights under the share option scheme. The court held that he was not entitled to damages for the loss of his option to purchase shares and that it was valid for the company to exclude its liability in respect of the share option scheme by the express terms of the contract. Mr Micklefield had also tried to rely on the Unfair Contract Terms Act 1977 in order to establish that the exclusion of the company's liability in respect of the option scheme was unlawful. The court held that the Unfair Contract Terms Act did not apply because the share option scheme was a contract for the creation of securities and was therefore exempt.

A different result was reached in *Chapman v Aberdeen Construction Group plc* [1991] IRLR 505. This case involved a similar rule in a share option scheme which excluded the executive's right to damages or compensation in the event of dismissal. However, section 23 of the Unfair Contract Terms Act 1977 (which only applies in Scotland) operated to make the exclusion clause void. Accordingly, Mr Chapman successfully claimed damages in respect of loss of rights under the share option scheme.

In *Clark v BET* [1997] IRLR 348 Mr Clark did not recover compensation for loss of share options. Mr Clark had already exercised his share options up to the maximum allowed under the BET Scheme prior to his dismissal, and had sold the shares. Mr Clark claimed that having done this, he was entitled to further options. The court held, however, that Mr Clark's employment contract only allowed him to exercise the share options he had already been granted.

A recent Court of Appeal decision in *Levett* v *Biotrace International plc, The Times*, May 1999 established that an employment contract which provided for the executive's share options to lapse if the contract was terminated was valid only if the company lawfully terminated the executive's employment contract. In this case, it was accepted that the company had terminated Mr Levett's contract unlawfully. The company could not then rely on its own breach of contract to bring the termination within the specific share option scheme rule which provided that the options would lapse on termination.

Although many share option schemes provide that rights under the scheme will lapse on termination of employment (either irrespective of the reason or for specific reasons) there is often a discretion to allow the executive's rights under the scheme to continue. Such a discretion, whilst not giving rise to a right to damages, will often feature in the severance negotiations.

6.6 Other claims/heads of loss

Following an assessment of the executive's loss by reference to his remuneration, it may be important to check whether the executive has any other potential heads of loss (excluding for the moment statutory rights such as unfair dismissal or discrimination). Such rights do not necessarily arise from the executive's employment contract but may enhance the amount of damages payable. One potential claim which will be referable to the employment contract will be where there has been a breach of a contractual termination or disciplinary procedure. However, can the executive claim damages for other potential claims such as injury to feelings or to reputation or compensation for loss of job security?

Injury to reputation

Until recently, it would not have been possible for an executive to recover damages for injury to his/her reputation caused by his employer. As mentioned earlier, in *Malik & Another* v *BCCI* [1997]

IRLR 462 the House of Lords established the principle that an executive may recover damages for loss arising from damage to reputation caused by the employer's breach of the implied term of mutual trust and confidence (see Chap 2). In the particular circumstances of the case, BCCI's breach was to have conducted its business in a dishonest manner, thereby potentially adversely affecting the employees' future employment prospects.

However, whether compensation is recoverable in such circumstances will depend on the executive being able to prove not only loss, but also that the loss was caused by the breach of the implied term of trust and confidence. The issue here is not whether employment is terminated wrongfully (*i.e.* without notice or pay in lieu of notice) but whether the employer's conduct (including the manner of dismissal) causes damage to the executive's reputation leading to financial loss. Whilst the circumstances in the *Malik* case were unusual, the principle of stigma damages is not necessarily confined to situations where the employer is operating a corrupt business. For example, an executive who is dismissed for gross misconduct (perhaps linked with suspected criminal activity or financial irregularity) where the employer has not acted reasonably, may suffer loss if he is not able to obtain future employment due to the stigma which arises as a result of the manner of the dismissal.

Note also that an executive may have a claim for loss where the employer has made defamatory remarks or statements. This could potentially arise when providing a reference. Employers, in any event, owe a duty of care to the executive when preparing a reference and to ensure it is accurate. The executive may claim damages if this duty is breached and the breach gives rise to loss (*Spring* v *Guardian Assurance plc* [1994] 3 All ER 129).

Injury to feelings

Whilst *Malik* establishes that an executive may recover compensation for damage to reputation, it is still not possible to claim damages for injury to feelings. Whilst a breach of trust and confidence which causes loss by making it difficult for the executive to obtain future employment can be compensated, an executive cannot claim damages for hurt feelings arising from the manner of termination (*Addis* v *Gramophone Company* [1909] AC 488, HL).

Loss of employment security

In a recent case (*Nicholson* v *Budget Insurance Ltd*, judgment of 8 June 1998) it was held that an executive cannot claim damages for loss of job security. Mr Nicholson gave up one job and took up his employment with the company on the understanding that the post was likely to be permanent. He was dismissed without notice or pay in lieu for alleged gross misconduct but did not have the two years' service necessary to bring an unfair dismissal claim. Although the EAT felt the gross misconduct allegation was unfounded it was not prepared to build on the *Malik* case by awarding damages for loss of security of employment.

Breach of contractual procedure

Where the employer has a contractual disciplinary procedure which it fails to follow, can the executive recover damages for this breach? The answer is yes. However, although damages are intended to put the executive into the position he would have been in had the breach not taken place, in cases of breach of a contractual disciplinary procedure this will be limited to lengthening the damages period to the period of time it would have taken to follow the procedure. It will not compensate the executive for loss of the chance that had the proper procedure been followed he would not have been dismissed. This was the outcome in *Janciuk* v *Winerite Ltd* [1998] IRLR 63, EAT. The EAT said that to compensate for loss of a chance that there would have been no dismissal involved consideration of the concept of fairness. Whilst this is relevant in the statutory claim of unfair dismissal, it is not relevant in breach of contract claims.

6.7 Further increasing value of severance package

The amount of the severance package is not usually limited to a valuation of potential claims and negotiations solely in relation to these. Employers often add to the overall package in other ways. The most common of these includes meeting all or part of the executive's legal or other professional fees in relation to the termination of his employment, providing outplacement consultancy and paying an additional sum as consideration for the executive to accept new post-termination restrictions.

New restrictions

Note that consideration for restrictions may be necessary to prevent the entire termination payment being taxable (see below). Accordingly, although in such circumstances a sum may be expressly referred to in the severance agreement as consideration for entering into new covenants, it is not necessarily the case that the consideration need be a sum in addition to the severance payment. In fact, often it will be part of the total planned severance payment which is just earmarked as consideration for new restrictions.

Outplacement consultancy

The provision of outplacement consultancy has become increasingly common. It is generally an additional item included in the package; it is rare that an executive will accept that the provision of outplacement should be taken into account in deciding whether his legal entitlements have been paid in full. The provision of outplacement consultancy advice is exempt from tax provided that:

- outplacement (described as qualifying counselling services in the relevant legislation is provided to the executive in connection with the termination of employment;

- the main purpose of the outplacement is to enable the executive to adjust to the termination of employment or to assist in finding other employment (including self-employment) or both;

- the outplacement consists of all or any of the following, namely, giving advice and guidance, imparting or improving skills, and providing or making available the use of office equipment or similar facilities;

- the executive has been employed by the employer full-time for two years ending at the time when the outplacement is provided or, if earlier, at the date of termination of employment;

- the opportunity to receive outplacement on similar terms is available to other executives/employees of the employer; and

- the outplacement is provided in the United Kingdom.

Legal and professional fees (and Part 36 offers)

As part of a settlement negotiation, an employer may be willing to meet either all or part of the executive's legal and other professional fees in addition to compensation for loss of salary and benefits. In relation to legal fees this has tax advantages for the executive as any sums expressed to be payable in respect of legal fees are exempt from tax (this was set out in an Extra Statutory Concession published in September 1993). This may be particularly relevant and a useful negotiating tactic where the total severance package is just over £30,000. By attributing the amount which exceeds £30,000 to legal fees the executive may be able to ensure that no tax is payable on the severance package.

It is now standard practice for employers to agree to pay a small amount of money for legal costs where the executive has been asked to sign a compromise agreement to waive statutory rights. As explained in Chapter 5 the compromise agreement is one of the binding ways in which an executive can waive his statutory employment protection rights and the waiver will not be valid unless he has received independent advice on the terms and effect of the agreement before signing it. Following changes introduced by the Employment Rights (Dispute Resolution) Act 1998 such advice may be provided by either a qualified legal adviser or certain individuals belonging to either an independent trade union or an advice centre (see Chap 5). In most cases the executive's advice will be from a qualified legal adviser and therefore a contribution to legal fees is likely to be part of the negotiation.

Contributions by the employer to legal fees may be affected by Part 36 offers under the Civil Procedure Rules (CPR) (see Chap 5). Where the employer makes a Part 36 offer prior to proceedings and the employer is likely to be the defendant if proceedings are issued, the employer must as part of the offer agree to meet the executive's legal costs for the period up to 21 days after the date the offer is made. An offer is made when it is received by the recipient. Note that in this context, the employer is not obliged to meet all the executive's costs without limit. Rather, costs must be proportionate to the case and the issues involved and costs will be assessed on the standard basis.

This marks a significant change in the employer's negotiating position. Whereas prior to the CPR the employer could decide as part of an overall negotiation whether to make any contribution to legal fees and if so, the amount of contribution, now the employer, in relation to a Part 36 offer is obliged to offer to meet legal fees. Further, pre-CPR, a contribution to legal fees usually formed a term of a compromise agreement (which settled both contractual and statutory claims). Part 36 offers, however, relate only to contractual claims. Where an executive has both contractual and statutory claims, in order to settle the latter an employer will still potentially need a compromise agreement and may find in the context of a negotiation that a contribution to legal fees is a term of the compromise agreement in addition to the offer to meet legal fees made in the context of a Part 36 offer.

6.8 Taxation of severance payments

Whether payments made on termination are taxable is an important issue in any severance negotiation. Further, it is not a straightforward issue to address as the tax liability varies according to the nature of the particular payment. Set out below are the main principles which should be applied in relation to the tax treatment of some of the main payments made on termination.

Note that the main legislation governing the tax treatment of termination payments is the Income and Corporation Taxes Act 1988 (ICTA)

General principle

Under section 19 of the ICTA income tax is payable on the emoluments of an office or employment. Emoluments includes salaries, fees, wages, perquisites and profits. Therefore, as a general rule, payments made on termination pursuant to a contractual obligation will be taxable as an emolument. This is irrespective of how the employer and executive choose to describe the payment in the severance agreement. Contractual payments which will be taxable include:

- pay in lieu of notice paid pursuant to an express contractual pay in lieu of notice clause or paid in accordance with the employer's custom and practice (giving rise to an implied contractual pay in lieu of notice provision);

- golden parachutes;
- compensation in relation to restrictive covenants paid pursuant to a contractual term (see further the section on restrictive covenants below);
- terminal or loyalty bonuses. These are payments which the employer may make conditional on the executive meeting certain targets, providing continued service/loyalty after receiving notice of termination or managing a handover of client connections to the employer's satisfaction. The Inland Revenue may, using this principle, seek to tax in full severance payments which are agreed some months in advance of an agreed termination date, arguing that the payment is actually pursuant to the contract of employment or varied by this agreed arrangement.

Not all contractual entitlements will be taxable, however (see below on redundancy).

Particular situations – what tax exemptions apply?

Although the general rule is that contractual payments will be taxable in full, there are situations where tax is not payable in part or at all on termination. The relevant statutory provisions governing the taxation of termination payments are section 148 and Schedule 11 of the ICTA. Section 148 of the ICTA sets out a general rule that tax is payable on any payment (not otherwise chargeable to tax, *e.g.* under the general charging provision of s19, ICTA) made in connection with the termination of employment or an office. However this is subject to the following exceptions

£30,000 tax-free

The main exception is that the first £30,000 of any payment to which section 148 applies is not taxable. Amounts in excess of £30,000 are taxable at the appropriate rate (see further below).

Death, injury or disability

Tax is not charged on *ex-gratia* payments made on the death of an executive and payments made to executives whose employment is terminated due to serious injury or disability (see Inland Revenue Statement of Practice SP 10/81 for the Revenue's interpretation of these terms) are wholly exempt from tax. However, if the Revenue can identify any parts of the payments which are contractual, tax may still be payable on those parts as emoluments of the employment under section 19 of the ICTA.

Foreign service

If the executive has been working or has worked outside the United Kingdom for one year or more, full or partial tax relief may be available as provided for in Schedule 11, ICTA.

Retirement

Ex-gratia payments made on retirement or in anticipation of retirement are fully taxable unless the payment is made pursuant to a contractual retirement scheme designed to provide a tax-free lump sum on retirement which has been approved by the Inland Revenue. It can be difficult to ascertain whether or not a termination payment is for early retirement, particularly where the executive is older. The Inland Revenue will look at each case individually. Although it is not possible to determine categorically what will amount to retirement, where the executive is near retirement age and unlikely to gain future full-time equivalent employment, the Inland Revenue is likely to argue that the termination payment is made in anticipation of retirement and is therefore all taxable unless it is made pursuant to an approved scheme. However, there may be circumstances (for example, the termination is just one in a large redundancy programme) where the Inland Revenue will accept that it is not paid in respect of retirement (*i.e.* the £30,000 exemption would be available).

Redundancy

Where the termination is due to redundancy, any statutory redundancy entitlement is exempt from tax (s 579, ICTA) but must be counted towards the £30,000 exemption. Many employers have enhanced redundancy schemes and payments under these may also qualify for relief following the decision of the House of Lords in *Mairs* v *Haughey* [1993] IRLR 551 but only to the extent that when aggregated with other payments made on termination (including statutory redundancy pay) the total falls within the £30,000 exemption. Following this case the Inland Revenue issued Statement of Practice (SP1/94) which provides that lump sum payments which are made in addition to or instead of statutory redundancy pay will only be liable to income tax under section 148 of the ICTA (and will therefore benefit from the £30,000 exemption) provided they are genuinely made solely on account of redundancy, as defined in the Employment Rights Act 1996. The Statement of Practice provides that this exemption will apply whether the scheme is an express contractual scheme or whether it is an ad hoc or improvised scheme designed to meet a specific situation.

Wrongful dismissal

Where there are no grounds for instant dismissal, but employment is terminated without notice or pay in lieu of notice and the executive receives damages for this wrongful dismissal, the damages are not taxable except to the extent they exceed £30,000. As damages are calculated on a net basis (to reflect what the executive would have received had he been allowed to work the notice period or balance of the fixed term as the case may be) the executive will effectively suffer two lots of tax deductions in respect of the excess over £30,000. Accordingly, as was held in *Shove* v *Downs Surgical* (referred to above) damages, although calculated on a net basis, should be grossed up to reflect the tax which the executive has to pay so leaving him with the net amount as originally calculated.

Restrictive covenants

Quite often, an employer will wish either to reaffirm existing post-termination restrictions on the executive's activities or to make an additional payment in return for the executive's agreement not to compete for an agreed period. The Inland Revenue has argued that such payments are fully taxable (s 313, ICTA). The Revenue's approach was clarified by the Inland Revenue's Statement of Practice SP3/96 which confirmed that there will be no taxable value if the executive reaffirms existing post-termination restraints. However, payments made to executives for new restrictive covenants entered into on termination will be taxable in full under section 313 ICTA without the benefit of the £30,000 exemption.

Where a severance agreement includes fresh restrictive covenants there is a risk that the Revenue will treat all sums payable under the agreement as taxable. The agreement, therefore, should identify any payments for new post-termination restraints. Although it may be tempting to attribute only a nominal value to the restrictive covenants in order to minimise the taxation consequences for the executive and the national insurance liabilities for the executive and the employer (see below), this may have an adverse effect on the enforceability of the covenant. The courts can consider the amount paid in return for a restrictive covenant when determining whether the covenant is reasonable and enforceable (*D* v *M* [1996] IRLR 192).

Applying the £30,000 exemption and making PAYE deductions on termination

Applying the £30,000

Where the £30,000 tax exemption is available, it must be applied as follows:

- to earlier tax years before later tax years; and
- in any tax year to cash before non-cash benefits.

These rules are best explained by way of example:

- an executive whose employment terminates on 31 December 1999 agrees to a severance package of total cash of £40,000 (half payable on the termination date and the other half on 1 May 2000) and retaining the company car (which is new and has a list price of £20,000) until 1 May 2000;
- as at 31 December 1999 the employer does not have a PAYE liability as the first tranche of the cash (£20,000) is within the £30,000 exemption. Further there is no PAYE liability in respect of the provision of the car;
- as at 1 May 2000 the employer will have a PAYE obligation. To ascertain this liability the employer should take account of how the £30,000 exemption has been used up. Applying the £30,000 exemption in accordance with the above principles the employer should:
  (i) first take account of the £20,000 cash paid on 31 December 1999;
  (ii) then take account of the taxable benefit of the car for the 1999/2000 tax year (as tax years must be considered individually with cash before non-cash in each tax year).

The relevant period is 1 January 2000 to 5 April 2000 (95 days). The taxable benefit of the car is:

£20,000 (list price) x 35% x 95 days) ÷ 365 days = £1,821.92;

(iii) this leaves £8,178.08 of the exemption (£30,000-£21,821.92) to be applied to the second tranche of the cash payment of £20,000 payable on 1 May 2000. The employer's PAYE obligation is to pay tax at basic rate (23%) on £11,821.92 (£20,000-£8,178.08) *i.e.* tax of £2,719.04 should be deducted. The executive must declare the benefit of the car from 6 April 2000 to 1 May 2000 under self-assessment.

Applicable tax rate

Generally, the employer must deduct and account to the Inland Revenue for tax under PAYE on the excess of the termination payment over £30,000 (assuming the £30,000 exemption is applicable). The rate at which tax is deducted differs according to whether the termination payment is made before or after the issue of Form P45:

After
If the termination payment is made after Form P45 has been issued, the payment should not be included in the P45 and tax should be deducted at basic rate. This is arguably the case even where the agreement which gives rise to the termination payment is concluded prior to the issue of the P45.

Before
If the termination payment is made before Form P45 is issued, the P45 should refer to the taxable element of the termination payment; the tax which should be deducted by the employer should be by reference to the executive's tax code for the particular year.

Notification to Inland Revenue

Regulation 23 of the Income Tax (Employment) Regulations 1993 provides that on termination of employment the employer is obliged to issue a P45. Copies of this are to be sent to the executive and the Inland Revenue. An employer may incur financial penalties for failure to comply with this Regulation. In respect of terminations after 6 April 1998 where the total remuneration package exceeds £30,000, the employer is required to submit a further return to the Inland Revenue prior to 6 July after the tax year in which the cessation took place (Income Tax (Employment) (Amendment) Regulations 1999). This notification should include details of the termination package including the cash and non-cash benefits provided and identify the tax years in which they were paid or enjoyed.

National Insurance implications

Where a termination payment can be regarded as being contractual (*i.e.* made pursuant to a contractual pay in lieu of notice clause or other provision in the contract such as a golden parachute), it will constitute "earnings" and National Insurance contributions will be payable in respect of it. Payments in respect of restrictive covenants also constitute "earnings" for National Insurance purposes. Genuine *ex-gratia* payments, compensation for loss of office and redundancy payments are not treated as earnings and, accordingly, do not attract National Insurance contributions.

Remember that both the employer and the executive have separate National Insurance liabilities. For the executive there is a weekly ceiling (currently £500 of earnings per week) and if a contractual termination payment is paid in a single sum, the National Insurance liability for the executive will be the National Insurance due on this weekly earnings limit. However, for the employer there is no weekly limit; employers' National Insurance (currently at 12.2%) will be due on the entire payment. Any contract for the executive to reimburse the employer for its (not the executiveís) liability to National Insurance is unenforceable

6.9 **Mitigation/accelerated receipt**

Once the executive's net loss (*i.e.* gross value of salary and benefits which would have been paid/received for the notice period/balance of fixed term less tax and national insurance) has been calculated, there may be adjustments to take account of mitigation, accelerated receipt and contingencies.

Mitigation

Whilst there is a duty on the executive to mitigate his loss by seeking alternative employment, mitigation is often a contested element of any executive severance and is particularly relevant to directors of institutions or public companies (see below).

The court considers two issues in relation to mitigation, namely:

(1) Has the executive taken reasonable steps to mitigate his loss to date? and
(2) What are the chances of the executive obtaining alternative employment between the date of the hearing and the expiry of the notice period/balance of fixed term?

In the *John Clark* case, the court found that Mr Clark had taken adequate steps to obtain alternative employment up to the hearing date. This was on the basis of correspondence Mr Clark had entered into as part of his search for employment and the evidence of a head-hunter whom Mr Clark had contacted the day after his dismissal and regularly thereafter. Interestingly, however, the court accepted Mr Clark's evidence that "if you push too hard, you become damaged goods" as an acceptable explanation as to any gaps which existed in his correspondence relating to his job search and accepted that Mr Clark should not have to lower his sights, as far as future employment opportunities were concerned. In addition, the court accepted evidence that appointments of individuals aged 55 and over to the type of senior position being sought by Mr Clark were rare and that he was more likely to obtain some non-executive directorships. On this basis, the court applied a total mitigating sum of £90,000 over the remainder of the notice period.

Accelerated receipt

A deduction should be made for accelerated receipt, to reflect the fact (where relevant) that the termination payment will be received in one lump sum earlier than it would have been received as salary. The longer the period of compensation the more relevant such a deduction will be.

Key points

When assessing the value of the severance package bear in mind the following:

- what are the executive's net earnings during the notice period/balance of the fixed term?
- is the executive contractually entitled to any increases in salary

during the notice period/balance of the fixed term?

- is the executive entitled to any commission/bonus (remember to look at the terms of any relevant bonus scheme and to take into account the issue of how any discretion to award bonus should be exercised)?

- has the company got a contractual pay in lieu of notice provision in the contract (check whether it is limited to basic salary or whether it also covers contractual benefits and possibly bonus)?

- does the executive have a company car (is there any private as well as business use?)

- check the position in relation to accrued holiday;

- what is the executive's pension entitlement and how will the company assess loss?

- does the executive have any entitlement to be compensated for loss pursuant to the terms of a share option scheme (check whether or not the company has lawfully terminated the contract)?

- has the executive got grounds to argue that there has been damage to his reputation?

- are there any contractual claims arising from any failure to follow a contractual procedure (whether disciplinary or severance)?

- will the £30,000 exemption apply to any severance payment?

- will the company offer to provide outplacement counselling or to bear any legal or other professional fees?

- remember to take account of mitigation and accelerated receipt.

Chapter 7

Protection of Business Interests

7.1 **Introduction**

Executives have usually obtained considerable knowledge of sensitive commercial information during their appointment and often have influence with key business contacts, such as suppliers, and customers. When effecting the termination of an executive's employment, companies should consider carefully the impact this may have on their business, and the means by which damage to the interests of the company can be minimised.

This chapter outlines the duties which an executive owes the company, both during employment and after employment has terminated. An awareness of these issues should assist companies in preparing the paperwork when severing an executive's employment and in deciding the appropriate strategic approach to be adopted in any particular case. For example, where an executive has no post-termination restrictions in his employment contract, but is in a position to jeopardise key customer contacts, it may be appropriate for the company to rely upon a garden leave clause (if there is one) in the employment contract (see below) or to negotiate suitable post-termination restrictions.

When effecting the termination, companies should be careful to remind executives of their duties to the company during the notice period (if applicable), or following termination of employment. These issues should be addressed in the severance documentation in order to avoid argument arising from uncertainty in the event that the executive breaches any of his obligations.

Key points

- whilst employed, executives are impliedly under certain duties during the course of their employment. To impose more extensive duties upon employed executives or to exert any control over the activities of ex-executives, express agreement is required;
- as a matter of public policy, contractual restraints applying after termination of employment will only be upheld where they are reasonably required for the protection of the company's legitimate business interests;
- neither past nor present executives may misuse confidential information belonging to the company, whether or not their contracts expressly prohibit them from doing so;
- the scope of what is considered confidential diminishes considerably once employment ends.

7.2 **Activities while employed**

Confidential information

The question of what constitutes confidential information was considered by the Court of Appeal in *Faccenda Chicken Ltd* v *Fowler* [1986] ICR 297 which concerned a sales manager who formed his own company and recruited several of the ex-company's van salesmen. Use was made of their knowledge of their old sales routes, the identities and needs of their customers, and of the company's pricing policies.

Three categories of information were identified by the Court:

- trivial or publicly accessible information;
- information which is obviously confidential but which the executive can use after termination because it forms part of his skill and knowledge base ("second category information"); and
- specific trade secrets which cannot be used after termination of employment.

In the circumstances of *Faccenda*, it was held that the knowledge which Mr Fowler was using after employment in competition with the company was not in the nature of a trade secret. Instead, it fell into the second category of information, being confidential information which should be respected by the executive during employment, but which could not be protected by the company post-termination.

When deciding into which category the information falls, the court will consider the following factors:

(1) Did the executive work in a job where he regularly handled confidential information? If so, he may more readily be expected to recognise and respect its sensitivity;
(2) Did the company impress upon the executive the confidentiality of the information (this may often be taken as a matter of common sense)?
(3) Could the allegedly confidential information be readily isolated from other information which the executive was free to use?
(4) How restricted was the circulation of the information within the business?

Expanding the category

What should a company do where the executive is not intending to abuse trade secrets, but will use general confidential information? It has been said that restrictive covenants cannot be used after employment ends to prohibit the use or disclosure of information which is not truly a trade secret and falls within the secondary category referred to above (*Faccenda Chicken*). However, this has been questioned in a number of cases and it is now generally considered that a suitably drafted covenant in the executive's employment contract or severance documentation may help to make it clear that particular categories of information are indeed treated as confidential. This will assist a company seeking to protect the confidential information by way of an injunction or damages (see below).

Client contacts

Companies are commonly concerned about the extent to which client details can be protected. The case of *Wallace Bogan* v *Cove* [1997] IRLR 453 concerned solicitors setting up in practice, in competition with their former employer. It was held in that case that the home addresses of clients were not confidential information, the use of which an employer could restrain after employment irrespective of the nature of the employment. Had this information been exploited during employment, however, the position would have been quite different.

Such activity on the part of the solicitors would have amounted to a breach of the express or implied duties owed by them to their employer.

Breach

Breach of confidence is unlawful and it is not confined to the duration of the employment relationship alone. Both current and former executives are under an implied obligation not to use or disclose information if it amounts to a trade secret or is so highly confidential that it requires the same protection as a trade secret. As *Faccenda* makes clear, however, second category information is not generally protectable after employment has terminated.

Whilst employed, executives are prevented from disclosing or using second category information, (*i.e.* information which is confidential but not to such an extent as to amount to a trade secret). Such secondary category information may be used by ex-executives to the extent that they inevitably carry it away in their heads. This does not mean, however, that information is not a trade secret merely because it is so carried away.

The obligation not to disclose trade secrets is, in principle, one of unlimited duration. However, a time is likely to come when the information loses its confidential character, either because it becomes out of date, or because it enters the public domain (*i.e.* it has become known to a substantial number of people). Third parties to whom confidential information is disclosed, whether lawfully or otherwise, also become bound by the obligation unless they have given value for it, and have not been put on notice that it is being transmitted in breach of confidence.

Implied terms

The executive, in his position as both an employee and officer of the company, owes his employer a number of implied duties, while he remains employed, which essentially mean that he must not do anything which would have an adverse affect on the company's business. The duty to act in the interests of the company and not for any collateral purpose is commonly known as the "fiduciary duty". This duty is outlined in Chapter 2.

Directors are also under a statutory duty to comply with the relevant provisions of the Companies Act 1985, which include a duty to disclose personal interests in contracts with the company, restrictions on loans, and provisions relating to the director's share dealings. Directors of listed companies must also comply with the requirements contained in the Stock Exchange's Yellow Book, but these issues are beyond the scope of this book.

It will not normally matter that the activities to which objection is taken are carried out in the executive's spare time, if they are such as to harm the company's business.

Breaches of these implied or statutory duties may justify summary dismissal at common law and constitute grounds for fair dismissal. They will also, in appropriate circumstances, enable the company to seek an injunction preventing an executive from working for a rival business until all or part of his notice period has expired (see below).

Preparing to compete

There is authority to the effect that an executive who merely takes steps in his own time towards being able to compete with his employer after the employment ends is not in breach of contract. Nonetheless, the submission of a tender for work in rivalry with his employer is unlawful competition and, it seems, would be so even if the executive was prepared to time giving contractual notice so it expires before work arising from the tender was due to start.

It is arguable that directors may not even prepare to compete unless they resign from the board first. This argument, however, did not find favour with the court in *Balston Ltd* v *Headline Filters Ltd* [1990] FSR 385 which held that preparation to compete was not a breach of the executive's duty of good faith.

As can be seen, when considering implied duties the line between legitimate and illegitimate activities is a fine one and the company's HR professionals and advisers should take care to spell out the nature of the executive's implied duties to the company during the notice period in any severance documentation. In most cases, it is also worth ensuring that the executive agrees to keep both the terms and existence of any severance terms confidential. Some wording is suggested in the compromise agreement at Appendix C, page 123.

Express terms

Companies frequently wish their executives to enter into express covenants restraining them from engaging in competing activities during their employment. Such executives may also enter into positive obligations to devote their whole time and attention to the company's business and negative obligations not to undertake any other business profession or occupation during their employment.

It is also increasingly common for employment contracts to contain comprehensive garden leave provisions which can be of considerable practical use to companies seeking to protect business interests when terminating the employment of executives.

What is garden leave?

Under the employment contract the executive may be excluded from the office and required to perform no duties or only to perform certain duties for the whole or part of the notice period. The executive receives full pay and benefits for the duration of the notice period but is prevented from either working or providing services to anyone other than the company who is still paying his salary. Instead, the executive has an opportunity to catch up on the garden!

When can the company rely on garden leave?

The company is able to hold the executive to the notice period when either the executive or the company seeks to end the employment relationship by giving contractual notice to the other. A company may also opt for garden leave where the executive seeks to resign, in breach of contract, with immediate effect. Here, the company may choose whether or not to accept repudiation of the contract by the executive and allow the executive to leave or to refuse to accept the breach and treat the contract as continuing.

The advantages of garden leave

Garden leave may have a number of advantages for the company:

- the company's confidential information may be out of date (or forgotten) by the time the executive is released onto the job market and free to join a new company;

- the company has time to find an appropriate replacement and the replacement has an opportunity to develop relationships with the departing executive's clients and business contacts;
- the executive is denied access to the company's remaining staff, records, computer system etc;
- the new company faces a delay before the executive arrives, as well as the potential risk that the departing executive's clients may not follow him;
- there may be no post-termination restraints in the employment contract or there may be post-termination restraints but there is a danger that they will be unenforceable. In these circumstances, garden leave provides a useful alternative means of achieving some protection of business interests;
- courts are prepared to re-write garden leave provisions, whereas restrictions applying after termination of employment will not be re-written: they must either be enforceable/ reasonable or they will fail (see below);
- as the employment contract continues during the period of garden leave all of the executive's express and implied duties of employment relating to confidentiality and fidelity continue and are enforceable, if necessary, by injunction. This is advantageous as the implied duty of confidentiality covers a considerably wider range of the company's business information while employment continues than after termination. This may be important where the executive possesses information which would be useful to a competitor but which might not fall within either the contractually agreed categories of protected information or the definition of protectable confidential information after termination of employment.

Garden leave does, however, have certain disadvantages:

(1) The company must continue to pay full salary, provide benefits and meet national insurance contributions during the period of garden leave when the executive may be wholly or largely unproductive.

(2) The executive accrues holiday entitlement whilst at home on garden leave. Whilst this may be of minimal importance for executives with relatively short notice periods, it can increase the cost of keeping executives with long notice periods and high salaries on garden leave since it is common for employment contracts to require the company to make a payment in lieu of accrued but untaken holiday on termination of employment (see further, below, as to whether the

company can require an executive to use up accrued holiday during garden leave).

(3) Garden leave offers little protection if an executive's notice entitlement is short.

(4) To attempt to put an executive on garden leave for the entirety of a long notice period may amount to an unreasonable restraint. Companies should therefore be prepared to be flexible in negotiating severance arrangements.

Example

Provident Financial Group v Hayward [1989] ICR 160

Mr Hayward was the financial director of the Provident Financial Group's estate agency business, Whitegates Estate Agency. He gave notice of resignation in July 1988 to accept employment as a financial controller with a rival chain of estate agents, ASDA Property Services. His contractual notice period was 12 months but it was agreed that his employment would terminate on 31 December 1988. He worked until early September 1988 at which time his company put him on garden leave. On 13 October Mr Hayward announced that he would be commencing work for ASDA on the following Monday and Provident sought an injunction to restrain him from doing so.

The relevant provision in Mr Hayward's contract of employment stated that during his employment he would not:

> "undertake any other business or profession or be or become an executive or agent of any other person or persons or assist or have any financial interest in any other business or profession ..."

Provident argued that the injunction should be granted to restrain Mr Hayward from working for anyone else or, alternatively, if this was too wide, that the injunction should be granted in a more limited form restraining Mr Hayward from working for their competitors. Mr Hayward argued it was not possible for the court to reduce the scope of the wide restriction in his contract. The court said that any company is entitled to prevent an executive from working for its competitors in breach of the executive's duty of good faith, irrespective of whether the duty is expressly spelled out in the contract (but see *William Hill* v *Tucker*, below). The courts could, in effect, "re-write" an unreasonably wide clause preventing an executive from working for any business so that it was reasonable and only applied to working for competitors.

Whilst the Court of Appeal recognised the principle of garden leave, it refused to grant an injunction for the following reasons:

- whilst the business of both the old and new companies was selling houses, they each relied on a different custom. Whitegates operated from high street premises and relied on custom from the street whereas ASDA operated out of ASDA supermarkets and relied on supermarket customers for business;
- there was no serious risk of detriment to Provident if an injunction were not granted. The executive's new position was in financial administration and given that Mr Hayward was a financial controller who had never enjoyed personal contact with customers, he did not have any confidential information that would be relevant to ASDA.

The Court of Appeal said that where the confidential information in an executive's possession would be highly prejudicial to the company if he worked for a rival, it might be correct to uphold a restriction preventing the executive from doing so until the expiration of a reasonable period of notice.

The message for companies is that it is not enough simply to include an express garden leave clause in the contract of employment. An injunction will only be granted to enforce garden leave if the company can convince the court that its business will be damaged if the executive begins working for a competitor during the notice period. This may be particularly difficult if the executive has already started working for the competitor by the time the case is heard and there is only a short time remaining of the notice period (which is commonly the case).

How to decide?

Companies should consider the following issues before deciding whether to put the executive on gardening leave:

- whether the executive is going to join a competitor;
- whether or not the company's goodwill or other business interests will be affected adversely by the executive being able to join the new employer immediately;
- whether the executive will use his skills upon taking up new employment to further the success of a competitor;
- whether or not damages would be an adequate remedy (*i.e.* could the loss be quantified in monetary terms?);

- the detriment (if any) which the executive will suffer if an injunction is granted.

It should also be remembered that the court should only grant such relief as is necessary to protect the company from damage which will be suffered if the notice period in the contract is disregarded. The notice period should therefore be long enough to be of some practical assistance to the company, but not so long as to be unreasonable. In light of the recent case law and the recommendations contained in the Combined Code on Corporate Governance (June 1998), garden leave in respect of notice periods in excess of six months is likely to be difficult to enforce.

Is an express clause necessary?

There are no reported cases in which the court has been prepared to enforce garden leave in the absence of an express term preventing the executive from working for anyone else during his employment. In the recent case of *William Hill Organisation Ltd* v *Tucker* the Court of Appeal held that whether an executive who had given notice to terminate his employment could be restrained from working while being paid his remuneration during the notice period depended largely on the terms of the contract of employment.

In the absence of an express clause or negotiated agreement on termination, therefore, companies may not be able to put executives on gardening leave. Companies should, therefore, include an express garden leave clause in executives' employment contracts or negotiate the terms governing garden leave in severance documentation. The clause should provide for:

(1) The right to require the executive not to attend work or undertake any work during the notice period (whether notice has been given by the company or the executive).
(2) The right to require the executive to perform no duties or duties other than his or her usual duties, at the company's discretion.
(3) The executive must not be employed by or provide services to any competitor during the garden leave period (consider whether non-competing activities will be permissible with the company's express written consent and whether the contract should end in such circumstances or at least whether the company should have a right to stop paying the executive).

(4) The executive must receive full salary and enjoy all contractual benefits during the garden leave period.

(5) Whether or not the executive will receive profit share or bonus during garden leave (this will depend on the terms and nature of the scheme).

(6) The right of the company to require the executive to take accrued holiday entitlement during the notice period and that if put on garden leave, the executive is deemed to be using up holiday entitlement which would otherwise accrue up to the actual termination date below (although note that in *Whittle Contractors Ltd* v *Smith*, EAT, 842/94 the employee was entitled to be paid for holiday which accrued during two months he spent on garden leave despite an express contractual term stating that holiday was deemed to be taken whilst the employee was on garden leave).

(7) A prohibition on the executive having any contact with colleagues, clients or suppliers/other third parties without the company's express written consent (NB: consider potential problems arising from social contact and client - initiated contact);

(8) The right to require the executive's resignation from directorships and other offices held by him (for example, trustee of an occupational pension scheme) as from the beginning of the garden leave period. In the case of executives who are entitled to attend board meetings, this final point is important since if, as a result of the garden leave, the executive is unlawfully prevented from attending board meetings, he may be able to terminate the employment contract and claim constructive dismissal.

A suggested clause is contained at Appendix B, page 122.

Is the garden leave clause incorporated in the contract?

Where an employment contract is amended to include a garden leave clause, it is important that the executive signs the amendment. If the executive does not, he may later be able to argue that the garden leave clause is not validly incorporated into the contract and, accordingly, cannot be upheld.

Policing garden leave

The executive's implied and express duties continue during the period of garden leave which should prevent the executive from taking steps actively to approach other employees or clients. In practice, however, it is often very difficult for the company to police the activities of the executive once he is out of the office. Furthermore, even after a period of time spent in the garden, it may be that the executive's customer contacts will follow him to a new employer. For these reasons, companies sometimes prefer to keep the executive in the office during the notice period and to vary his duties under the garden leave clause in order the minimise contact with confidential information/customers. A carefully worded clause will enable the company to take a flexible approach in order to meet the circumstances of each case.

Summary of considerations

- Is the executive in a position to threaten the company's legitimate business interests? If so:

- Would it be preferable to have the executive in the office, or at home on garden leave?

- Is there an entitlement under the employment contract to put the executive on garden leave? If not, should the company negotiate that arrangement? If so, an additional payment may be necessary.

- How long is the notice period and will it be enforceable? If not, should the company agree a shorter period of garden leave?

- Remind the executive of his express and implied duties pending termination of employment and that a breach could result in summary termination.

- Ensure that the executive has resigned all offices held in the company.

- Ensure that all confidential information/company property is returned.

- Make payment under severance terms conditional upon compliance with the above.

7.3 Activities after employment

In addition to restrictions on the executive's activities during employment, the company may seek to rely on restrictions applying after termination. Again, the aim is to protect legitimate business interests, such as goodwill, confidential information and business contacts. Post-termination restrictions in the employment contract must do no more than is reasonably practicable to protect those interests or they will be void as being in restraint of trade.

Types of restrictive covenant

Non-solicitation covenants

These prohibit the former executive from soliciting the custom of clients or customers of the company. While the cases conflict on the point, such restraints are most likely to be upheld if the pool of prohibited clients is limited to those with whom the former executive dealt personally within a defined and reasonable period immediately preceding the termination of his employment. Note that in all cases the prohibited pool of clients should not include those who became customers only after the ex-executive's departure since these would not form part of the company's existing legitimate interests during the executive's employment.

Non-dealing covenants

These prohibit the former executive from dealing with clients or suppliers of the company, irrespective of whether the ex-executive initiated the approach. The restriction is greater than that imposed by non-solicitation covenants but may be justified where a non-solicitation covenant would be impossible to police. In practice, the courts are often willing to accept that to prove solicitation by the ex-executive would impose too great a burden on the company, so making reasonable a covenant of the non-dealing type. Problems often arise where clients or suppliers are also on social terms with the ex-executive and consideration should be given to this issue when drafting both employment contracts and severance documentation.

Non-competition covenants

These prohibit the former executive from being engaged by or interested in a competitive activity. Typically, such restrictions are drafted as area covenants defined by reference to a radius taken from the company's place of business, or a territory or region which reflects the scope of the executive's duties or the company's activities. However, care should be taken to ensure that area restrictions are not too wide or irrelevant (where, for example, the business is international). It is often preferable to identify specific rival businesses. The same principles apply to either form. Such covenants are difficult to enforce because they can severely limit the executive's activities in his chosen industry and the law will only uphold them against ex-executives if they are justified. Such justification has been found to exist in two classes of situation:

(1) Where the executive has access to confidential information. There will be implied (if not express) prohibitions on the use and disclosure of such information after employment, but these prohibitions are notoriously difficult to police and even the most honest executive may break them inadvertently. Provided that the information is capable of causing real damage in the hands of a competitor, the courts will therefore accept it as a basis for an appropriately limited non-competition covenant. The courts take an increasingly broad view of what constitutes protectable information, *e.g.* marketing strategies or other business plans, if sufficiently concrete, have been accepted. However, it remains the case, as indicated above, that information which is in the nature of the executive's general skill and knowledge is not protectable.

(2) Where customers, although regular, are not readily identifiable or where their solicitation by the ex-executive would be difficult to detect.

A common objection to non-competition covenants is that their effect may be to prohibit an ex-executive from some innocuous activity, such as joining a competitor in a wholly non-competitive area of its business or in a role where knowledge of the former employer's information or customers would be irrelevant. Consider, therefore, when drafting such covenants limiting the scope of the prohibited activities accordingly. In addition, ensure that an executive who was engaged in one particular sector of an industry is not subjected to a covenant excluding him from participation across the whole of that industry.

Non-solicitation of other executives

The validity of restraints on "poaching", *i.e.* the recruitment by an ex-executive of his former colleagues, is increasingly accepted by the courts, if the company can show an investment in a complement of skilled staff. Such a covenant is likely to fail if it applies to all employees regardless of their expertise or seniority. Remember also that the covenant must protect existing business interests, and so a clause will not be enforced to protect employees recruited after the executive has left the company.

Indirect restraints

The rule that restraints going beyond the reasonable protection of legitimate interests are void applies to indirect as well as to direct restraints. For example, the Court has struck down a provision that outstanding commission would not be paid after the termination of employment if the executive joined a competitor.

How long should the restraint last?

For all the above restrictions a key factor in deciding their enforceability will be the period for which they are intended to apply after termination of employment. As a rule of thumb, the shorter the restriction the more likely it is to be enforced. A restraint of a year or less is likely to be easier to justify than one of more than, say, two or three years' duration. Careful consideration should be given to the interest being protected and the actual (rather than perceived) protection required by the company.

The drafting of restrictive covenants is a matter upon which companies should seek specialist advice. The enforceability of covenants depends on the circumstances of each case. In addition, drafting of other parts of the contract can affect the validity of covenants.

Interpretation

In construing restrictive covenants the courts apply the following tests:

- covenants must be clearly drafted or they may be held void for uncertainty;
- the reasonableness of the covenant is often said to be judged at the time when the contract is concluded. However, in practice its reasonableness must also be shown at the time it is sought to be enforced, in order to persuade a court to grant an injunction;
- covenants will not be rewritten by the court to make them enforceable;
- an unenforceable covenant or part of a covenant may be "blue

pencilled" or severed, provided that what is left makes independent sense without the need for modifying the wording and that the sense of the contract is not changed;

- it is considerably easier to uphold a covenant if it forms part of the agreement on the sale of a business by the person restrained, even if that person is also an executive;
- where restrictive covenants are entered into between parties who each carry on business in the supply of goods or services, they may be subject to the regime of control imposed by the Restrictive Trade Practices Act 1976, from which certain exemptions are made by Restrictive Trade Practices (Sale and Purchase and Share Subscription Agreements) (Goods) Order 1989 (SI 1989 No 1081). A full explanation of these provisions is beyond the scope of this book;
- in *Morris Angel & Son Ltd* v *Hollande* [1993] ICR 71, it was held that after the transfer of an undertaking a restrictive covenant should be read as being enforceable by the transferee, but only in respect of customers of the transferor who fall within the protection.

Effect of wrongful dismissal

If the company dismisses the executive in breach of contract (which will generally be because the requisite notice has not been given), or if the executive resigns in response to the company's repudiatory breach of contract, the company will not be entitled to enforce any restrictive covenants contained in the contract. This is because a party to a contract cannot benefit from the terms of a contract which it has breached.

In this context, to dismiss an executive and pay him in lieu of notice may amount to a breach of contract unless either there is contractual provision allowing the company to adopt this course or the executive consents to it. Thus, although the pay in lieu would ensure that the executive had no outstanding claim in damages, the breach would allow him to escape from the restrictive covenants.

Enforcement

The purpose of a carefully planned and executed executive severance is, among other things, to avoid the need for litigation. If, however, a company needs to threaten or bring proceedings there are two basic remedies which may be sought where a restrictive covenant is breached or there is a misuse of confidential information.

Damages

A claim may be brought against the executive for breach of contract or breach of confidence. Also, it may be possible in an appropriate case to sue his new company for inducing a breach of contract or for breach of confidence. The problem with this course of action is that it may often be very difficult to prove what loss has occurred because the executive will argue that, for example, the customers would have transferred to a competitor in any event. Further, the executive may be unable to meet an award of damages.

An injunction

The most effective remedy which a company can obtain is an injunction restraining the ex-executive or executive from breaking the express or implied terms of his contract or misusing information in breach of confidence. An application may be made for an interlocutory injunction (*i.e.* before trial of the action) and this is usually the decisive stage in any legal proceedings.

Applications for injunctions should be made as soon as evidence of a breach has come to light.

Whether or not an interlocutory injunction is granted will depend upon whether the company can show an arguable case that it will succeed at trial, that it would not be adequately compensated by an award of damages at trial (*e.g.* because of the difficulty of proving loss), and upon the court's assessment of where the *balance of convenience* lies.

The court should only resort to an attempt to assess the merits of the rival claims at the interlocutory stage if the restraint will have expired or largely expired before the action can be tried. This approach will tend to favour the company, because (where the balance of convenience is otherwise even, as it often is) the court will tend to preserve the status quo by restraining the executive.

Company property

Where there is good reason to believe that the executive may have in his possession property belonging to the company or copies of information confidential to the company, it is common to seek further orders in addition to the basic injunction. One such order is for the delivery up of the items in question.

Alternatively, the company could apply for a search order: a type of injunction which instructs the executive to allow the company's representatives access to particular premises in order to search for such property or for defined categories of documentary evidence. This is a draconian order and one which is seldom made by the court. The court will have to be persuaded that it is likely that the property is on the premises and that, without such an order, there is a real risk that it will be destroyed, hidden or tampered with, with serious results for the company's ability to enforce its rights.

Confidentiality

If the executive has by some wrongful act (*e.g.* the copying of confidential information whilst still employed) obtained an advantage or "springboard" in competition with the company, an injunction may be granted in such form as will neutralise that unfair advantage, *e.g.* the ex-executive may be prevented from competing in certain ways for a specified period of time until the confidential information loses its sensitive character. This type of order is known as a springboard injunction.

It has been said that a "springboard" order cannot be used as a means of depriving the executive of future benefits where that would put the company into a better position than if there had been no breach of confidence.

A company which applies for an injunction must be prepared to give a cross-undertaking in damages, that is, an undertaking to make good loss caused to the executive if he eventually proves that the order should not have been made.

Inducing a breach

It is not unlawful for one company to poach the employees of another, unless that company encourages the employee to breach terms of his contract with the existing employer (whether the terms relate to confidentiality, notice or post termination restrictions).

In practice, the poaching company is usually careful to distance itself from any breach of contract. It is common for the "poacher" to write a letter to the executive confirming that any employment is subject to the executive giving the current employer notice, and confirming that he would not be in breach of any express or implied duties to the current employer in accepting the offer made by the "poacher".

Where there is evidence that the "poacher" was aware of the executive's contractual obligations, however, and still encouraged him to act in breach, a claim may be brought against the subsequent employer for damages for inducing a breach of contract.

One way of strengthening the company's hand is to insert a clause into the employment contract or severance documentation obliging the executive to inform any subsequent employer of the restrictions applying to him both during and after termination. Then if those restrictions are breached the company can assume either that the executive has failed to inform his new employer of the restrictions (a breach of contract) or that the new employer knew and turned a blind eye.

Commercial deterrents

The practical impact of garden leave or restrictive covenants can be bolstered by the inclusion in the employment contract or severance documentation of a liquidated damages clause, pre-estimating the loss which would be suffered by the company in the event of a specified breach of contract. Such a clause may give the departing executive, and any "poaching" company second thoughts.

Such clauses should be drafted carefully, however, since if the amount provided is too low the poacher may consider the risk commercially advantageous, whereas if the amount is too high, it may be construed as a penalty clause (*i.e.* the effect is to prevent a breach rather than to provide a genuine pre-estimate of loss). Penalty clauses are unenforceable under English law.

Key points

Does the company wish to protect business interests after employment has terminated? If so:

- Has the employment contract been terminated lawfully? If so:

- Are there any post termination restrictions in the employment contract? Do they meet the company's concerns?

- Are they reasonable to protect existing legitimate business interests?

- should alternative covenants be negotiated as part of the severance arrangements?

Remember to:

- Remind the executive of his duties and the consequences of non-compliance.
- Consider making payment conditional on compliance.

Duties Summary	
During employment	*After employment*
Executive	*Executive*
■ Confidentiality (includes second category information) ■ Duty of fidelity ■ Fiduciary duties ■ Duties under the Companies Act 1985 ■ Express terms (not to compete/to devote attention and time to interests of the company) ■ Garden leave	■ Confidentiality (limited to trade secrets, where no express clause has been agreed) ■ Restrictive covenants: - non-competition - non-poaching of employees - non-solicitation of clients/suppliers - non-dealing with clients/suppliers
Employer	*Employer*
■ Trust and confidence ■ Health and safety ■ Payment of emoluments	■ To give an honest reference (duty owed to both the executive and his subsequent employer)

Appendix A

Letter Confirming Dismissal

[Employer's Headed Notepaper]

[name]
[address]

[date]

Dear [name]

I am writing to confirm our discussions [today/on [date]] when I informed you of [my/the Company's] decision to terminate your employment with [immediate effect/effect from [date]] (the Termination Date) and of the reasons for that decision.*

[You are entitled to [amount] months' notice. The Company will pay you £[amount] (less deductions for tax and national insurance contributions) in lieu of your notice period on the Termination Date.]**

Yours sincerely

for and on behalf of
[Company's name]

* *The company may wish to specify the reasons for dismissal, particularly where the executive has a statutory right to written reasons for dismissal.*

** *There will be no need to give notice or pay in lieu of notice if the company has grounds to effect instant dismissal.*

· Garden Leave Clause ·

If either you or the Company serves notice on the other to terminate your employment or if you indicate an intention to terminate your employment without notice the Company may require you to take garden leave for all or part of the notice period. You will continue to be paid and enjoy your full contractual benefits during any period of garden leave.

During garden leave the Company may in its absolute discretion:

(1) exclude you from the premises of the Company or any associated company;
(2) require you to carry out specified duties (consistent with your status) for the Company or to carry out no duties;
(3) require you to resign immediately from any offices you hold in the Company or any associated company;
(4) require you to return to the Company immediately all documents and other Company property;
(5) instruct you not without the prior written permission of the Company to contact or attempt to contact any client, customer, supplier, agent, officers, employees or representatives of the Company or any associated company.

Appendix C

· Compromise Agreement ·

[Employer's Headed Notepaper]

SUBJECT TO CONTRACT
WITHOUT PREJUDICE

[Name of Executive]
[Address]

[date]

Dear [**Name**]

I write to you on behalf of [**name of employer**] ("the Company") to set out proposals for dealing with the termination of your employment with the Company and your directorship or any other offices which you have with the Company or any Group Company with effect from [date] ("the Termination Date").

In this agreement the following expressions have the following meanings:

"Group Company"	means any company or other organisation which is directly controlled by the Company or which directly or indirectly controls the Company or which is a successor or assign of the Company;
"the Employment Legislation"	means the Employment Rights Act 1996, the Disability Discrimination Act 1995, the Sex Discrimination Act 1975, the Race Relations Act 1976, the Trade Union and Labour Relations (Consolidation) Act 1992 and the Working Time Regulations 1998 all as amended by the Employment Rights (Dispute Resolution) Act 1998.

1. Salary

1.1   You will be paid your accrued salary up to and including the Termination Date, together with a sum in lieu of holiday accrued but not taken (both amounts being subject to deductions for tax and national insurance).

1.2 You will be reimbursed for all expenses reasonably incurred by you in the proper performance of your duties in accordance with the Company's policy and subject to delivery of your expenses claim form to me no later than [date].

2. Termination Payments

2.1 Provided you have signed and returned the duplicate of this agreement and sent me your signed adviser's Certificate, the Company will, within 14 days of the Termination Date, pay you £[   ] (the Termination Payment) as compensation for the termination of your employment with the Company.

OR

2.1 The Company will pay you [£   ] (the Termination Payment) as compensation for the loss of your employment with the Company. The Termination Payment will be paid in [   ] instalments of [£   ] per month, on or about the last date of each month. If you obtain new employment or self employment prior to [date], the Termination Payment will be reduced by your earnings from that date, as evidenced by your payslips or invoices.

The Termination Payment will be subject to deduction of tax and national insurance (as appropriate) before it is paid to you.

2.2 The Company will pay your [**reasonable**] legal fees in connection with this matter direct to your solicitors, (name of firm) [up to a maximum of £[   ] [including/excluding] VAT and disbursements within [14] days of receiving their invoice.

3. Resignation as a director

3.1 You will resign as a Director of the Company and any relevant Group Company by signing the letter of resignation in the form annexed hereto.

3.2 From the date of your resignation as a director you agree you will not conduct yourself in any way which is inconsistent with having surrendered your authority.

4. Statements and confidentiality

4.1 The Company will, promptly on request from a prospective employer, provide you with a reference in terms of the draft annexed hereto.

4.2 You will not make, or cause to be made, any derogatory or critical comments or statements which may reasonably be expected to lower the reputation of the Company, or any Group Company or any of their respective officers or employees.

4.3 You agree, without limit in time, not to publish or make use of, directly or indirectly, any trade secrets or confidential information belonging to the Company, or any Group Company including but not limited to business plans, customer lists, financial information, research plans, sales and marketing programme [**list any other relevant items**].

4.4 You further agree to keep the terms and existence of this agreement confidential and not to disclose them to any other person or oganisation, save for professional advisers or where required by law.

5. Pension

You will receive a statement of your accrued benefits under [**name of company pension scheme**] and the options available to you following termination of your employment.

6. Company car

You may retain your existing Company car, registration [   ] until [**date**] on the current basis [**save that you will be responsible for maintenance and running costs, including petrol expenses**]. You will maintain the vehicle in good working order and not do anything to vitiate any policy of insurance. You must return the Company car, together with all keys and documents relating to it, to me at the Company's premises on [**date**].

7. Tax

7.1. Save for tax or national insurance already deducted by the Company you will be responsible for the payment of tax and national insurance (if any) arising by reason of the Termination Payments [or benefits] referred to above. [**The Company believes that the first £30,000 of the Termination Payment may be made to you free of tax and national insurance**].

[7.2 You agree to indemnify the Company against any tax or national insurance as referred to in paragraph 7.1 above (whether or not the Company is primarily liable to the relevant tax authority in respect of the liability in question).]

8. Company property

You will [immediately] [within 7 days of the Termination Date] return to the Company property in your possession and control, including [**list any relevant items**].

9. Settlement

9.1. This agreement is made without any admission of liability on the part of the Company [or any Group Company] in full and final settlement of all and any claims, proceedings or rights of action whatsoever and howsoever arising which you have or may have against the Company, or any Group Company, or any of their officers or employees relating to your employment or directorship of the Company, or any Group Company, or the termination thereof.

9.2. To give full effect to the provisions in paragraph 9.1 above you:

9.2.1. agree to refrain from instituting or continuing any proceedings before an Employment Tribunal in relation to any claims or complaints within the Employment Legislation;

9.2.2. agree, in particular, but without limiting the general nature of paragraph 9.2.1 above, to refrain from instituting or continuing any proceedings before an Employment Tribunal for:

[include specific complaints];

9.2.3. confirm you have received advice from a relevant independent adviser as defined in the Employment Legislation concerning the terms and effect of this agreement and, in particular, its effect on your ability to pursue your rights before an Employment Tribunal;

9.2.4. confirm that your adviser has provided you with evidence that there is in force a contract of insurance or an indemnity provided for members of a profession or professional body covering the risk of a claim by you in respect of loss arising in consequence of the advice;

9.2.5. agree that the conditions regulating compromise agreements in the Employment Legislation are hereby satisfied.

Please sign and return to me the duplicate of this agreement together with your Adviser's certificate and letter of resignation of directorships.

Yours sincerely

. . . .

[   ]
for and on behalf of the Company

I understand and accept the above terms. I further agree to compromise all and any claims under the Employment Legislation and/or arising from or relating to my contract of employment with the Company or the termination thereof. I acknowledge that I have obtained legal advice from [name] of [name of firm] as to the terms and effect of this agreement and in particular on my ability to pursue a claim in the Employment Tribunal. I have received a certificate from my adviser confirming that all conditions regulating compromise agreements under the Employment Legislation are satisfied, and a copy of that certificate is attached at Schedule 1.

. . . .

NAME OF EXECUTIVE   DATED

Schedule 1

Adviser's certificate

I hereby certify as follows;

1.   I am a relevant independent adviser as defined in the Employment Legislation as referred to below.
2.   I have advised [insert name of executive] of the terms and effect of the agreement between [his/her] employer, [insert name of employer], and [him/her] dated _____ and, in particular, its effect on [insert name of executive]'s ability to pursue a claim before an employment tribunal following its signing.
3.   There is in force a contract of insurance or an indemnity provided for members of a profession or professional body covering the risk of a claim by [insert name of executive].
4.   I confirm that the conditions regulating compromise agreements under section 203(3) of the Employment Rights Act 1996, section 77(4A) of the Sex Discrimination 1975, section 72(4A) of the Race Relations Act 1976, section 288 of the Trade Union and Labour Relations (Consolidation) Act 1992, section 9(3) of the Disability Discrimination Act 1995 and regulation 35(3) of the Working Time Regulations 1998 all as amended by the Employment Rights (Dispute Resolution) Act 1998 (together "the Employment Legislation") are satisfied by the agreement.

SIGNED: . . . .
ADVISER: . . . .
FIRM NAME: . . . .
ADDRESS: . . . .
                  . . . .
                  . . . .
                  . . . .
REFERENCE: . . . .
DATED: . . . .

For advisers other than qualified lawyers insert a new paragraph 3 as follows:

[3.   I have written confirmation of competency to give this advice and am authorised to do so by [insert name of trade union/advice centre]. I enclose a copy of that confirmation and authorisation. [For advice centres only:] I confirm that no payment has been made to me by or on behalf of [insert name of executive] in relation to this advice.]

and renumber remaining paragraphs.

Calculation of Wrongful Dismissal Damages

	£	£
Gross annual loss of salary and taxable benefits		
Salary (any assumed right to annual increases?)	60,000	
Bonus/Commission	30,000	
Car (use Inland Revenue car scale rate)	----	
Other benefits (*e.g.* medical expenses insurance for executive at cost to the Company)	400	
Total gross salary and taxable benefits		94,400
Deduct:		
Employee's pension contributions (at 5% of salary)	3,000	
Single person's tax allowance (1999/2000)	4,335	
Miscellaneous tax allowances (if applicable)	----	
	7,335	
Total taxable salary and benefits	87,065	
Tax (1999/2000 rates):		
10% on first £1,500	150	
23% on £1,501–£28,000	6,095	
40% over £28,000	23,626	
	29,871	
Deduct:		
Total tax	29,871	
NIC (1999/2000 rates assuming contracted in rate)	2,257	
	32,128	
		62,272
Add:		
Nontaxable benefits (if any)	----	
Net annual loss of salary and benefits		62,272

	£	£
cf Net annual loss of salary and benefits		62,272
Net loss over notice period		
£62,272 x 18 months 12		93,408
Modifications		
Deduct:		
Mitigation of loss (no deduction to illustrate a worst case scenario)	----	
Accelerated receipt and contingencies (discount at 3%)	2,802	
net loss over notice period after modifications		90,606
Tax on payment		
Amount to be grossed up	90,606	
Less tax-free slice	[30,000]	
Taxable amount	60,606	
Tax payable (40/60 x 60,606)		40,404
ESTIMATED TOTAL AWARD OF DAMAGES (EXCLUDING PENSION LOSS)		131,018

Appendix E

Letter of Resignation of Directorships

The Directors
[**Insert company name**] Limited/PLC
[**List all companies from which**
the executive is to resign as a director]

[Date]

Dear Sirs

I hereby tender my resignation as a Director of the [**above-listed**] company[**ies**].

My resignation[s] [is/are] to take [immediate effect/effect on ....]

Yours faithfully

· Index ·

Absence abroad,
consequences of, 33
ACAS,
involvement of, 50, 59, 60
Agreement. *See* Compromise
agreement, Contract, Severance
agreement
Alternative employment,
mitigation of loss, through, 97
offers, effect of, 24
Announcements,
wording of, agreement over, 57,
58
Arbitration,
issues concerning, 59, 60
Articles of Association,
removal, under terms of, 33

Bankruptcy,
effect of, 33
Behaviour,
inconsistent behaviour, effect of,
27
Benefits. *See* Company car,
Pensions scheme, Private health
benefits, Share options
Bonus provisions,
employment contract, contained
in, 37, 54
remuneration provisions, as part
of, 78, 79
Breach of contract,
anticipatory breach, 21
damages, resulting from, 62
elements constituting, 18, 19
implied terms, existence of, 19,
20, 21
loss suffered, through, 76
procedural breach, effect of, 87
resignation following, 21
waiver, action constituting, 22
Business interests. *See* Protection of
business interests
Calderbank letter,

use of, 42
Civil Procedure Rules. *See also*
Woolf Reforms
effect of, 43, 89, 90
Claims,
settlement negotiations, 2, 41,
42, 43, 123 *et seq*
Client contacts,
protection of, 101
Commission for Racial Equality,
work of, 28
Company car,
remuneration package, as part
of, 80
retention of, 44, 55, 56, 125
Company interests. *See also*
Protection of business interests
costs and resources, consideration of, 40
precedent, action creating, 41
promotion of, obligations
relating to, 6, 8
Company property,
access to, 116
return of, 57, 125
Company reorganisation,
management considerations, 15
Compensation. *See also*
Compensation agreement,
Compensation awards
limits placed on, 2, 69, 73
Compensation awards,
discrimination, for, 28, 71
wages, deductions from, 72
Compromise agreement,
advantages of, 50
assistance, ongoing, provision
for, 59
company car, provisions for, 125
company property, return of,
57, 125
confidentiality, issues
concerning, 53, 58, 124
consideration, attached to, 53

departure statements, agreement
    over, 57, 58
holiday pay, provisions for, 54
meaning of, 49
parties to, 53
pension provisions, 125
salary provisions, 122
specimen copy, 123 *et seq*
statement, terms covering
    agreed, 124
structure of, 59
tax indemnity, given where, 57
tax provisions, 125
termination, date for, 52, 54
termination payment, provision
    for, 123
terms, contained in, 52, 125
use of, 50, 51
Conduct,
    behaviour, inconsistent, 27
    gross misconduct, effect of, 7
    obligations, relating to, 6
Confidential information. *See also*
    Confidentiality
    breaches, in respect of, 102
    disclosure, duties in relation to,
        102, 103
    fiduciary duties, exercise of, 102,
        119
    nature of, 100, 101
    protection of, 14, 15
Confidentiality,
    obligations, in respect of, 6
Conflicts of interest,
    avoidance of, requirements as to, 8,
        14
Constructive dismissal, 17 *et seq*
    breach of contract, effect on, 22
    claims for, 5
    grounds for, 18
    resignation, effect of, 22, 23
    time constraints, involved in, 18
Contract. *See also* **Breach of contract,**
    Employment contract, Fixed term
    contract
    implied terms, importance of, 19,
        20, 21
    relationship, created by, 1
    rights conferred by, 6
    temporary contract, dismissal
        where, 16
    termination of, dismissal following,
        5

Contributory fault,
    effect of, 68
Corporate governance,
    code of practice, 16, 108
Costs, 2, 62 *et seq*

Damages,
    calculation of, 62, 63, 93
    entitlement to, 7, 63
    "stigma" damages, 21
    taxable, whether, 93
Death,
    payments on, taxation of, 91
Director(s). *See also* **Directors' duties**
    employee, status as, 31
    removal of,
        articles of association, under, 33
        board of directors, by, 34
        shareholders by, 33, 34
Directors' duties,
    conflict of interests, avoiding, 8
    disclosure of information, by, 102,
        103
    good faith, acting in, 8
    summary of, 119
Directors' resolution,
    removal, by virtue of, 34
Directorship,
    resignation of, 4, 31, 32, 52, 57,
        131
    termination of, 31, 32, 52, 57
Disability,
    payments for, taxation of, 91
Disciplinary procedures,
    contract, included in, 7, 37
    fairness, requirement for, 20
    grounds for, 7
Discrimination,
    allegations of, dealing with, 27, 28
    compensation, awarded for, 28, 71
    direct discrimination, types of, 28
    indirect discrimination, types of,
        28, 29
    victimisation, 28
Dismissal procedures,
    costs related to, 1
    disclosure, changes related to, 2
    grounds for dismissal, 1, 7
    implications of, 1, 3
    qualifying periods, related to, 2
    reasonable action, company's
        obligations for, 8
    reasons for dismissal, analysis

required, 1
reforms, related to, 2,3
responsibility for dismissal, 1
"without prejudice" use of, 3, 4
Dismissal. *See also* **Constructive dismissal, Dismissal procedures, Unfair dismissal, Wrongful dismissal**
business considerations affecting, 15
circumstances leading to, 5, 6
director, employee's status as, 31
employment contract, attention paid to, 31
grounds for, 1, 7, 15, 16, 17
imprisonment, leading to, 17
interview, conduct of, 45, 46
letter of confirmation, 121
personality differences, leading to, 16
preparations for, 31 *et seq*
handling of, responsibility for, 45
strategic issues,
"best practice", following, 39, 40
clean break, effect of, 39
company objectives, 39
costs and resources, consideration of, 40
negotiating, creating space for, 41
precedent, action creating, 41
temporary contract, where, 16
third parties, requests from, 16
trust and confidence, breach of, 17
Documents,
disclosure of, rules affecting, 2
review of, advisable where, 35

Earnings,
loss of, consideration given to, 67
Employee's representatives,
negotiations with, 15
Employment contract,
bonus provisions, contained in, 37, 54
compromise agreements, related issues, 51, 52
directorship terminated, under, 32, 52
disciplinary provisions, contained in, 37
dismissal, provision for, in, 31, 63

garden leave, provisions contained in, 37
payment in lieu, provision for, 36, 40, 54
review of, advisable where, 35
unpaid sums, claims for, 65
Employment terms,
changes to, refusal to accept, 14, 15
Equal Opportunities Commission,
work of, 28
European law,
provisions of, 2
Ex-gratia payments, 52, 68, 91, 92
Executive. *See also* **Directors' duties**
company requests, compliance with, 6
definition of, 1
duties of, 6, 118
services provided by, 6
Expenses,
compliance with procedures, 6

Fairness at Work,
provisions governing, 1, 2, 67, 68, 69
Feelings. *See* **Injury to feelings**
Fiduciary duty,
breach of, 7
Fixed term contract,
termination of, 5
Formal warnings,
procedures involving, 10
Future loss,
bonus payments, loss of, 69, 70
consideration given to, 69
earnings, loss of, 69, 73, 75
employment prospects, consideration of, 69, 70, 74
period of loss, 73

Garden leave,
advantages of, 104, 105
assessing need for, 107, 108
contractual provisions for, 37, 104, 108, 109, 122
disadvantages of, 105, 106
draft clause, for, 122
nature of, 104
operation of, 106, 107, 119
policing of, 109, 110
reliance on, 104
Gross misconduct,
instances of, 7

Health benefits. *See* Private health
     benefits
Holiday pay,
     provisions for, 54

Illegality,
     executive position, resulting in, 13,
         14
Immigration provisions,
     adherence to, 14
Imprisonment,
     dismissal, following, 17
Independent professional advice,
     requirements as to, 49, 50, 128
Injury,
     payments for, taxation of, 91
Injury to feeling,
     awards made for, 28, 71, 86
Injury to reputation,
     consideration given to, 85, 86
IT equipment,
     retention of, 44

Job security,
     loss of, 87

Legal fees,
     contribution towards, 44, 53, 56,
         89, 90
Length of service,
     effect of, 26
Loss. *See* **Future loss**
Lost remuneration,
     assessment criteria, 77 *et seq*

Mental illness,
     effect of, 33
Misconduct, 7, 21
Mitigation of loss,
     obligations in respect of, 97

National Insurance,
     severance payments, implications
         for, 96
Negotiations,
     Calderbank letter, use of, 42
     compromise agreement, specimen
         copy, 123 *et seq*
     costs, considerations as to, 2
     creating space for, importance of,
         41
     defence position,

"on the record" negotiations,
     41, 42
"subject to contract"
     negotiations, 43
"without prejudice"
     negotiations, 41, 42
"without prejudice subject to
     costs" 42
offers,
     "on the record" offers, 43
     Part 36 offer, 43, 44, 89, 90
settlement, relating to, 2
tactics, involved in, 42, 44
Notice period,
     benefits, enjoyed during, 75, 76
     events occurring, during, 27
     length of, 74

Outplacement,
     counselling, provision of, 44, 56,
         88

Payment in lieu,
     contractual provisions for, 36, 40,
         54, 70
     taxation provisions, 90, 93
Pension rights,
     compromise agreements, covered
         by, 125
     earnings, limits placed on, 83
     entitlement, future, 82
     loss of, consideration given to, 67,
         69, 70, 81, 82, 83
Pensions scheme,
     payments into, 56
Power of attorney,
     directorship terminated, by means
         of, 32
Private health benefits,
     provision of, 44, 52, 56
Procedural safeguards,
     breach of procedures, effect of, 26
     codes of practice, observance of,
         25,
Procedure. **See Dismissal procedures**
Professional indemnity cover,
     requirement, as to, 49
Protection of business interests, 14,
     15, 39, 40, 99 *et seq*
     client contacts, protection of, 101
     commercial deterrents, impact of,
         117

confidential information, nature
of, 100, 101
executive's duty, company towards,
99, 100, 102
express terms, concerning, 104,
108
preparing to compete, 103

Redundancy. *See also* **Redundancy
payment**
business, closure of, 11
diminishing need, criteria for, 11
dismissal, relating to, 11
mergers, effect of, 13
statutory definition of, 11
workplace, closure of, 11
Redundancy payment,
calculation of, 12
consultation, obligations as to, 13
entitlement to, 12, 68, 92
tax, exemption from, 92
References,
requirements, as to, 53, 57
Relocation,
considerations relating to, 15
Remedies. *See also* **Damages**
injunction, application for, 115,
116
search orders, operation of, 116
Remuneration. *See also* **Earnings,
Future loss**
assessment criteria,
basic salary, 77
bonus payment, 78, 79
commission, 78
company car, 80
holiday pay, 80, 81
pension loss, 81, 82
Reputation. *See* **Injury to reputation
Resignation,**
consequences of, 21, 22, 124, 131
dismissal, leading to, 5
refusal by executive, 4
Restrictive covenants,
damages, claim for, 115
enforcement issues, 114
indirect restraints, 113
"inducing a breach", 116, 117
interpretation of, 113
non-competing covenants, 111,
118, 119
non-dealing covenants, 111

non-solicitation covenants, 111,
119
period of restraint, 113
"poaching", restrictions against,
112, 113, 116, 117
remedies, concerned with,
injunction, application for, 115,
116
search notices, operation of,
116
taxation, issues relating to, 93,
94
wrongful dismissal, issues
related to, 114
Retirement,
taxation of payments, on, 92

Service. *See* **Length of service**
Settlement. *See also* **Negotiations**
compromise agreement, specimen
copy, 123 *et seq*
tactics, relating to, 41, 42, 44, 89,
90
Severance agreement, 48 *et seq*. *See
also* **Compromise agreement,
Severance package,
Severance payments**
drafting of, 45
independent advice, requirement as
to, 49, 50
types of, 48
Severance package,
benefits, cost of providing
equivalent, 76
mitigation of loss, duties in respect
of, 97
reputation harmed, consideration
given to, 85, 86
value of, assessment of, 72, 73, 87
Severance payments,
accelerated receipts, effect of, 97
national insurance, implications
for, 96
taxation of, 88, 90, 91, 94, 95
Sexual harassment, 20
Share options,
loss of, compensation for, 84, 85
period for, extending, 44
Shareholders,
executive's status, as, 1, 34, 35
powers of, 35
removal by, directorship of, 33, 34

Shares,
    sale to company, whether required,
        34, 35
Staff morale,
    adverse effects on, 4,
    maintaining, importance of, 44, 45
Statements,
    departure, agreement as to, 57, 58
Statutory claims,
    settlement of, 52
Statutory provisions,
    implications of, 1, 6
Statutory rights,
    termination on, 65

Taxation,
    compromise agreement, provisions
        affected by, 125
    death, payments on, 91
    disability payments, 91
    ex gratia payments, 91, 92
    injury, payments for, 91
    redundancy, payment on, 92, 93,
        94
    retirement, payment on, 92
    severance payments, relating to,
        88, 90, 91, 95
    termination payment, of, 88
Termination. *See also* **Termination**
    date, Termination payment
    benefits, position on, 76
    PAYE deductions, on, 94
    post-termination restrictions,
        operation of, 53, 58, 93,
            110 *et seq*
    rights arising on, 62, 65
Termination date,
    agreement, as to, 52, 54
Termination payment,
    holiday pay, provisions for, 54
    instalment payments, 55
    provisions for, 54, 55
    tax exemptions, involving, 54
    tax liability, for, 88
Terms. *See* **Employment terms**
Theft,

accusations of, 20
Trade secrets,
    abuse of, 100, 101, 102
Trade Union,
    negotiations with, 15
Trust & confidence,
    breaches of, 17,
    implied terms, concerning, 19, 20,
        21
Unfair dismissal,
    claims for, 6, 23, 65, 66
    codes of practice, observance of, 25
    company resources, relevance of,
        24
    compensation, awarded for, 66, 67,
        68
    deductions from payments, 68
    fairness, criteria for, 23, 24
    inconsistent behaviour, leading to,
        27
    loss of earnings, consideration
        given to, 67, 74
    limits on payments, 69
    pension loss, assessing effect of, 83
    personal circumstances, mitigating
        factors, as, 27
    provisions governing, 2
    reasonableness, requirement for,
        23, 24
    remedies, available for, 66
    wrongful dismissal, relationship
        between, 70

Victimisation, 28

Wages,
    deductions from, 72
Woolf Reforms,
    effect of, 2, 3
Working Time Regulations,
    effect of, 80, 81
Wrongful dismissal,
    claims for, assessment of, 70, 73,
        74, 81
    damages for, 70, 129, 130
    loss, period of, 73, 81